The
Eternal Purpose

THE UNTOLD STORY OF HOW A HEAVENLY FATHER AND
HIS ONLY BEGOTTEN SON RESTORED MANKIND'S
INHERITANCE

*Jeanne :
Love you !!
Brad Mititala*

The

Eternal Purpose

THE UNTOLD STORY OF HOW A HEAVENLY FATHER AND
HIS ONLY BEGOTTEN SON RESTORED MANKIND'S
INHERITANCE

Bradley

Francis

Mehtala

ISBN-13: 978-1496155214
ISBN-10: 1496155211

eternalpurposebooks.com
Seattle, Washington

For Jaclyn

"THINE EYES DID SEE MY SUBSTANCE, YET BEING UNPERFECT; AND IN
YOUR BOOK ALL MY MEMBERS WERE WRITTEN, WHICH IN
CONTINUANCE WERE FASHIONED, WHEN AS YET THERE WAS NONE OF
THEM. HOW PRECIOUS ARE YOUR THOUGHTS UNTO ME, O GOD! HOW
GREAT IS THE SUM OF THEM! IF I SHOULD COUNT THEM, THEY ARE
MORE IN NUMBER THAN THE SAND…"

PSALM 139:16-18

"TO THE INTENT THAT NOW THE MANIFOLD WISDOM OF GOD SHOULD
BE MADE KNOWN TO THE RULERS AND AUTHORITIES IN THE HEAVENLY
REALM THROUGH THE CHURCH, ACCORDING TO THE ETERNAL
PURPOSE WHICH HE HAS PURPOSED IN CHRIST JESUS."

EPHESIANS 3:10-11

CONTENTS

INTRODUCTION

The Constitution of Creation

"FOR AS THE RAIN COMES DOWN, AND THE SNOW FROM HEAVEN, AND
DOES NOT RETURN THERE, BUT WATERS THE EARTH TO MAKE IT BRING
FORTH AND BUD, THAT IT MAY GIVE SEED TO THE SOWER AND BREAD
TO THE EATER, SO SHALL MY WORD BE THAT GOES FORTH OUT OF MY
MOUTH; IT SHALL NOT RETURN TO ME VOID, BUT SHALL ACCOMPLISH
WHAT I PLEASE, AND IT SHALL PROSPER IN THE THING FOR WHICH I
SENT IT."

ISAIAH 55:10-11

THE *JUDEO-CHRISTIAN* tradition[1] has always held to the view that from Genesis to Revelation the Holy Bible sets forth an accurate and dramatic history of events and interactions, both literal and emblematic, involving the natural realm and the spiritual realm, heaven and earth, good and evil, right and wrong -- man, angel, and God. We have often disagreed amongst ourselves on what is "literal" and what is "symbolic" in that history, but we are held together by the common belief that the essential chronicle or storyline, and yes even the *words themselves*, were indeed delivered from God to man as multiple authors recorded events and

---

[1] *See, generally, The Judeo-Christian Journal of Law & Theology (JCJ)* (www.juristheologica.com).

expressed their thoughts over the centuries as led or *inspired*[2] by God to do so.

Of course, those records, the very words and accounts provided by those who heard God's voice over the millennia, now make up the *"Canon of Scripture,"* the collection of writings we call The Holy Bible, and those writings have been (and will continue to be) a formative and fundamental element of our past, present, and future as a people. The last book of our Bible (Revelation) was written almost two thousand years ago; and, according to our faith, the narrative Moses provided in the first book of our Bible (Genesis) takes us all the way back to the very first human beings, to the very "womb of humanity" in *the Garden of Eden.* This has always been at the heart of the Judeo-Christian world-view, a world-view explicitly and implicitly founded on a particular record of events and characters, a history told through narrative, prophecy, and poetry dating back to a common beginning and ***therefore*** relevant and even ***essential*** to life itself.

So, for instance, from the moment of our humble beginnings to the modern world we live in, our own efforts at *justice, judgment, and law* have their roots and origins in experiences and interactions involving the God of the

---

[2] II Timothy 3:16

Bible and in stories and/or traditions involving those interactions as described in the Bible. Of course, the Judeo-Christian tradition and history present the clearest *manifestations* of this reality, but the influence of the scripture and of the *Word of God* doesn't stop with Western Civilization. As it is written: *"His judgments are in all the earth..."*[3]

Indeed, from the very beginning the light of God's own *jurisprudence* has provided a very real and practical *legal clinic* for mankind to observe and learn from as we have applied his standards and followed his examples in forming our *own* legal *relationships* with one another over the millennia. For instance, time and again we find the underlying values of *fairness, equity,* and *veracity* as the essential touchstones of God's own *"jurisprudential view"* as expressed in the scriptures. Through this lens we see our Heavenly Father's interest in *framing relationships,* relationships between himself and mankind, and among mankind as we deal with one another.

So Moses instructed, *"You shall not show partiality in judgment; you shall hear the small as well as the great; you shall not be afraid in any man's presence, for the judgment is God's. The case that is too hard for you, bring*

---

[3] Psalm 105:7-11

to me, and I will hear it."[4] And again, *"You shall do no injustice in judgment. You shall not be partial to the poor, nor honor the person of the mighty. In righteousness you shall judge your neighbor."*[5] And again, *"You shall not pervert justice; you shall not show partiality, nor take a bribe, for a bribe blinds the eyes of the wise and twists the words of the righteous."*[6] And finally, *"You shall do no injustice in judgment, in measurement of length, weight, or volume. You shall have honest scales, honest weights...."*[7] *"You shall have the same law for the stranger and for one from your own country; for I am the Lord your God."*[8]

The foregoing *principles* and the underlying values they express may look very basic -- but that begs the question. Because these original, beautiful, and organic statements of law, justice, and judgment are *verifiably* thousands of years old and their place in the history of the *"science of law"* cannot be questioned, especially in light of the fact that they were received by an audience (the children of Israel) who believed the words themselves *came from heaven*, from the *mind of God* written with the finger of God, the **ultimate** authority.

---

[4] Deuteronomy 1:17
[5] Leviticus 19:15
[6] Deuteronomy 16:19
[7] Leviticus 19:35-36
[8] Leviticus 24:22

And while these ideals seem old and even common now, they were "fresh new ideas" when first written, wildly progressive for their time and place. Consider, then, the *formative* force these organic ideas *must* have had on all those who read and/or heard them, from the time of Moses, through the people of Israel and the ancient world, through Church history, Rome, Catholicism, European history, Protestantism, the American Colonies, the United States, and then into the jurisprudential infrastructure of the secular West and even beyond. Looking for progressive notions of *equity* and *fairness*? Looking for a model *criminal* code, *bankruptcy* code, or law of *intestate succession* to prime the pump of justice? Just read from the five *Books of Moses* as a start – and we did.

From the beginning, God has been providing mankind with ample and interesting "*food for thought*" in the area of the *wisdom of law* and *jurisprudence*, and we have eaten of that food over the millennia. Generations of mankind have read from Moses, the Psalms, the Prophets, the Gospels, and the entire New Testament. The saturation-level of the source material is unequaled in history, crossing national and ethnic borders and covering thousands of years. The Bible was the first book ever printed and is **by far** the most widely published book in history, continuing to out-perform all others, world-wide.

And there in that Bible the whole time, between the lines of the *Ten Commandments* and the rules regarding clean and unclean meats, were those beautiful statements of *fairness, justice,* and *equity* ringing in the ears of generation after generation -- heard, digested, and reasoned through. You shall have the same law for the stranger and for those from your own country. You shall not show partiality in judgment; you shall hear the small as well as the great. You shall not be partial to the poor, nor honor the person of the mighty. You shall not pervert justice; you shall not show partiality. A bribe blinds the eyes of the wise and twists the words of the righteous. You shall have honest scales and honest weights. You shall do no injustice in judgment, in measurement of length, weight, or volume – settle out of court, turn the other cheek, go the extra mile.[9] This is the *jurisprudence* and *wisdom* of our God; we learned it all *from him.*

Just as the Wright brothers influenced aviation or Thomas Edison paved the way in electronics, the Bible's *noble ideals* governing how we *relate to* one another, and with God himself, have been *formative* and *instrumental* in providing guidance and light to untold numbers of decision-makers, policy makers, jurists, philosophers,

---

[9] *See, generally,* The Sermon on the Mount.

politicians, writers, teachers, coaches, parents, and presidents alike. The *principles* of *fairness* and *justice* ring as true today as they did a few thousand years ago when first heard, understood, and made *"the law of the land"* of Israel or *"the teachings of the Church"*[10] in the West -- no doubt *because* these seeds of *God's wisdom* have over the centuries become part of our collective thinking -- part of our cultural DNA. And where would we be *without them*? We tell our kids to be fair with one another, and we expect our bosses, our government, and *the law* to be fair to us. But who taught us to be fair? God did.

Two thousand years ago the Apostle Paul planted some of the most progressive *jurisprudential* seeds ever cultivated and brought to harvest when he said that "*in Christ*" there was *neither male nor female, Jew nor Greek, slave or free.*[11] No more categories; or at least *equal treatment* despite your category, which was *the whole idea*. This is just one beautiful example of the genius and power of God's *wisdom* at work in civilization as, through Paul, God planted *the seeds* of *gender and racial equality*

---

[10] *Note*: The idea of "The Church" was never meant to refer merely to the Catholic Church or any other denomination or sect; but rather, to "*the general assembly and church of the firstborn*" (Hebrews 12:23) -- all true believers throughout history irrespective of their label.

[11] Galatians 3:27-29. *Note*: the ideals set forth in this one scripture alone have produced, and will continue to produce, more *justice on earth* than we can possibly imagine.

in a culture, time, and place when such ideas were foreign, even radical. But those seeds contained their own unique power. Centuries later in America, the *Declaration of Independence* would declare that *"all men are created equal."* Later that *organic equality* was expressed as *legal equality* in the Fourteenth Amendment to the Unites States Constitution.[12]

But the intellectual history of *"equality and justice for all"* running from Moses through Paul's writing through *Church and European history* to the founding documents of the American Republic is not difficult to identify, not to mention how the *rest of the world* has been effected as the logic, wisdom, *and light* of ideals such as the *Golden Rule*[13] have gained *traction on earth* over the millennia. But let's never forget that it has been our Heavenly Father who has been spinning this thread, and shining this light, all along. The *secular* ideas and ideals we have employed in *governing ourselves and relating with one another* merely

---

[12] "All persons born or naturalized in the United States, and subject to the jurisdiction thereof, are citizens of the United States and of the State wherein they reside. No State shall make or enforce any law which shall abridge the privileges or immunities of citizens of the United States; nor shall any State deprive any person of life, liberty, or property, without due process of law; nor deny to any person within its jurisdiction the **equal protection** of the laws." Amendment Fourteen, United States Constitution.

[13] Matthew 7:12. The *Golden Rule*: "Do unto others as you would have them do unto you."

borrow from concepts originating in God's *own eternal wisdom*, a wisdom which has been *coming down from heaven* from the beginning. In fact, even the heavens *declare* the glory of God.[14]

So in his Epistle to the *Galatians,* Paul declared that despite race, ethnicity, class, and even gender all *"members"* of the *"body of Christ" were one* and had *equal standing* or legal rights before God as *"the seed of Abraham."*[15] In Ephesians Paul goes so far as to speak of a *new mankind*[16] in Christ, calling all that are *in Christ "fellow-citizens"*[17] of a whole new community or family. This wasn't Rome, Greece, Babylon, or even the nation of Israel; this was something new, a new *organization* of mankind! In this same vein the Apostle Peter refers to *the Church* as a *"holy nation"* under God.[18] The Pilgrims would ultimately bring these *concepts and ideals* to the *new world*, at least in theory.[19] So to some extent, these *principles* would eventually provide *the seeds* of the American *national identity* as *"one nation, under God, indivisible, with liberty and justice for all."* And while

---

[14] Psalm 19:1

[15] Galatians 3:27-29

[16] Ephesians 2:15

[17] Ephesians 2:19

[18] I Peter 2:9

[19] *Note*: This is about the ideas themselves, not the imperfection of man in applying them.

mankind has often failed miserably in applying God's values over the millennia, the point is that the values of God have still been there to guide us in the darkness. The God of the Bible may not always get the credit for *providing this light*, but that doesn't mean that the God of the Bible doesn't *deserve* that credit. So it is not, and never has been, America *per se* that has been a *beacon of light* in the world, but the *constellation of ideals* that America *declares* it is guided by. The ideals are *universal* – because they come *from heaven*.

In fact, after giving the people of **Israel** the "*statutes and judgments*" he **received** from *the hand of God*, Moses recognized the significance of *the example* they would set. As it is written, "*Surely I have taught you statutes and judgments, just as the Lord my God commanded me; that you should act according to them in the land which you go to possess. Therefore be careful to observe them; for this is your wisdom and your understanding in the sight of the Peoples **who will hear all these statutes**, and say, 'Surely this great nation is a wise and understanding people.'*"[20]

And we've just scratched the surface here. The *guidance* and *light* of God's *eternal wisdom* over the millennia has a broad and vivid spectrum, a spectrum that

---

[20] Deuteronomy 4:5-6

goes well beyond the general principles of *equality* and *justice* discussed so far.

For instance, God provided illustrative *hypotheticals* when teaching his people about justice and judgment, not unlike the hypotheticals law students, legal practitioners, and law-makers grapple with every day throughout the modern world. Legal reasoning, legal education, and legal analysis are forever indebted to this model. So the *great jurist* Moses writes *hypothetically* of someone who "*kills his neighbor unintentionally, not having hated him in time past, as when a man goes to the woods with his neighbor to cut timber, and his hand swings a stroke with the ax to cut down the tree, and the head slips from the handle and strikes his neighbor so that he dies....*"[21]

Here, we get a first glimpse into the *legal reasoning* behind the various degrees of homicide currently appearing in modern criminal codes -- an *unintentional* homicide distinguished from a homicide committed with *malice aforethought*. In yet another hypothetical Moses likens rape to murder: *"But if out in the country a man happens to meet a young woman pledged to be married and rapes her, only the man who has done this shall die. Do nothing to the woman; she has committed no sin*

---

[21] Deuteronomy 19:4-5

deserving death. ***This case is like that of someone who attacks and murders a neighbor.*** *"²²* This was a very *progressive notion* for its place and time -- that rape should be treated like murder – as a crime of violence. This was a good start for future legal analysis when it comes to the culpability involved in this horrible crime. It is also a fundamental indicator of a civilized society.

And the list goes on and on. The book of Jeremiah sets forth a fascinating example of early *property law.*²³ There we get to see all of the *elements* of a real estate transaction as a parcel of land is paid for, evidence of the transaction is witnessed and sealed, and documents are "recorded in a book" at the court. Still earlier, perhaps around 1444 B.C., Joshua encouraged Israel to *"go* ***possess** the land which the LORD God of your fathers hath* ***given you.*** *"²⁴* But Joshua also told them to *"go through the land and describe it."²⁵* So they did as they were told, as it is written: *"And the men went out and passed through the land and described it by cities into seven parts **in a book**... "²⁶* So here we are actually seeing a very early

---

²² Deuteronomy 22:25-26 NIV

²³ Jeremiah 32:7-16

²⁴ Joshua 18:3

²⁵ Joshua 18:4

²⁶ Joshua 18:9

example, *provided by God*, of formal *legal descriptions* officially recorded for public record.

In the Book of Numbers we see the intellectual seeds of the modern "*oath*," as well as the idea that a *contract* or *agreement* forms a legal "*bond*" that should remain unbroken.[27] Is it any wonder that this is the God who has himself used *covenants and promises* in his own interactions with man *from the beginning*? What did mankind learn from that *heavenly example*? The Book of Numbers also provides a remarkably detailed model for man's first law of *intestate succession or inheritance*.[28] But as we'll see, this was merely a foreshadowing of a law of *spiritual inheritance* that God had already *ordained from the beginning* for *his own children*.[29]

Of course, all of these examples may look antiquated to our modern eye; but perhaps a better word to describe them would be "*embryonic*." If modern man cheers the origins of life in science; why should we not also cheer the *origins of good law, good government, and justice*? But even more than being embryonic ideals for civilization, the truth is that all of these examples and many more reflect *spiritual realities* as well. They provide *a unique window*

---

[27] Numbers 30:2

[28] Numbers 27:1-11

[29] I will say much more on this later.

into the *nature and purpose of our Heavenly Father* as we see him in action and *learn about him* from what we hear and see.

So Esau *sold his birthright* to Jacob for a bowl of stew,[30] and God honored that transaction in *intangible property*. Similarly, during Messiah's temptation in the wilderness Satan claimed to have clear title to *all the kingdoms of this world*,[31] and our Savior did not argue with that claim. Paul tells us in Romans that *in Christ* we who were not children **become** children through *adoption*, which then *qualifies* us as *heirs*, and more specifically, *joint-heirs* with Christ.[32] So the truth is, there is an *underlying, unseen spiritual and jurisprudential reality* to all of this, and it has to do with the very *nature* of our Creator.[33] Once we understand this aspect of who he is, as well as understand how his creation and eternal purpose reflect this jurisprudential attribute, we will then know

---

[30] Genesis 25:31-33

[31] Luke 4:5-6

[32] Romans 8:17

[33] *Note*: When God put a *bow in the cloud* as a **token** *of his covenant* with man after the flood, he called that bow "*his bow*" (Genesis 9:13). This was God linking his own glory with a covenant or promise. So when Ezekiel saw a vision of the Throne of God, he identified a *bow of glory* around the throne, like "*the bow that is in the cloud on the day of rain*" (Ezekiel 1:28). Thus, God's *glory* is revealed in his *covenant-making*.

much more about ourselves, and how we fit in to that eternal purpose.

THE HABITATION OF JUSTICE

Our Heavenly Father was a "*Judge*" long before any human being came up with the idea of a judiciary. Similarly, God had his own idea of justice, fairness, equity, and even crime and punishment long before mankind began to wrestle with these noble ideals or put pen to paper in setting forth the law of the community he lived in. The interest in a "just balance, a just weight, and a just measure" did not find its first home in the heart and mind of man, but actually originated in the heart and mind of a God and Creator who, according to the Bible, made the *promise* of eternal life even before the world began.

God was "no respecter of persons" long before any man had the slightest glimmer of an idea of an equal protection clause. There was "*neither male nor female*" in Christ long before any human being began to fight for gender equality. God was making *covenants* long before man learned how to shake hands and make a deal. God had already decided to *adopt children* long before man thought of a way to apply the rights and privileges of *lineage* without the natural bond of a family/blood relationship. And finally, God had already set aside an *inheritance* for *his heirs* long before man considered the idea of passing his property upon death.

So while the scriptures attribute *many characteristics* to our Heavenly Father[34] -- God is Spirit, God is eternal, God is omniscient, God is immutable, God is invisible, God is everywhere present, and of course, God is love -- no other defining element or characteristic of *"who and what"* our Heavenly Father is permeates the scriptures *more deeply and broadly* than the fundamental idea that the God of Abraham, Isaac, and Jacob -- the God of the Bible -- is *just*. God is the very *habitation* of justice.[35] As it is written, *"Give ear, and I will speak; And hear, O earth, the words of my mouth. Let my teaching drop as the rain, my speech distill as the dew, as raindrops on the tender herb, and as showers on the grass. For I proclaim the name of the LORD: ascribe greatness to our God. He is the Rock, His work is perfect;* **for all his ways are justice***, a God of truth and without injustice; righteous and upright is he."*[36]

---

[34] Job 9:10; Romans 11:33. *Note:* These fundamental attributes of God describe His essential and distinctive person and nature and combine to inform our limited comprehension and understanding of a being who is, also by definition, "past finding out."

[35] Jeremiah 50:7

[36] Deuteronomy 32:1-4

Proverbs 16:11 reads: *"A just balance and scales are the Lord's; all the weights of the bag are His work."*[37] The Lexham English Bible has it: *"A balance and scales of justice belong to Yahweh; all the weights of the bag are his work."* So when we consider the *scales of justice* and all they symbolize, Proverbs 16:11 assures us that all of it *originates* in God.

All of God's ways *are justice*, and this is a theme that runs from Genesis to Revelation. God is, in fact, a *judge.*[38] God is a *lawgiver.*[39] God is the *habitation of justice.*[40] *Justice and judgment are the habitation of God's Throne.*[41] From the very beginning of time our Heavenly Father has described himself as the "Supreme Judicial Authority," a Sovereign Being occupied with the business of justice, judgment, law, equity, and the kind of wisdom, authority, and power that give meaning, certainty, *and life* to these noble and *eternal* ideals.

The truth is that from the profound *decrees* God issued in the *Garden of Eden* after the fall of man[42] to the climactic *unsealing of the scroll* God holds in his *right*

---

[37] Proverbs 16:11
[38] Genesis 18:25, Psalm 7:11
[39] James 4:12
[40] Jeremiah 50:7
[41] Psalm 89:14
[42] Genesis 3

hand in the book of Revelation,[43] the story of God, man, and even the angels, as told in the Bible, is predominantly a judicial and legal story. As it is written, *"...He has prepared his **throne for judgment**. He shall judge the world in righteousness; And He shall administer judgment for the peoples in uprightness."*[44] And again, *"Justice and judgment are the habitation of his throne."*[45]

Our Savior told the *legal practitioners* of his day: *"Woe unto you, scribes and Pharisees, hypocrites! For you pay tithe of mint and anise and cumin, and have omitted the **weightier** matters of the law -- judgment, mercy, and faith: these you should have done and not to leave the other undone."*[46] Our Messiah was telling those who handled the law that their *jurisprudence*, their analysis and application of law, was incorrectly *"weighted"* when it came to their emphasis (or lack of it) of *mercy, judgment, and faith* as compared to other priorities. He was telling the Scribes, Pharisees, and Lawyers -- you have the *scales of justice* in your hand, but you don't understand what they were supposed to teach you. So what is the *relative weight* of this ideal or that

---

[43] Revelation, Chapters 4 and 5.
[44] Psalm 9:7-8
[45] Psalm 89:14
[46] Matthew 23:23

ideal, this doctrine or that doctrine, or this issue or that – in the *mind and heart* of God? Where are God's priorities? What matters most to our Heavenly Father?

THE RELATIONSHIP

Nowhere was *a failure* in this regard more evident than in the trial of our *Beloved Savior* before the leaders and elders of Israel two thousand years ago in Jerusalem, a trial that involved the *legal issue of eternity*, the question of *the Relationship* Jesus of Nazareth had with his God, and that his God had with him. Consider again the final question put to our Savior at that trial, the question that would result in his crucifixion and death, and *therefore in our salvation*:

"I ADJURE YOU BY THE LIVING GOD THAT YOU TELL US WHETHER YOU ARE THE CHRIST, THE SON OF GOD?"

MATTHEW 26:63

Our Savior taught a parable about a man who owned a vineyard and lent it out to others to run for him when he was away. As the parable goes, the landowner was away for a long time, and sent ambassadors to see how the operation was going, but those ambassadors were treated shamefully. So the owner of the vineyard finally decided to send his *only Son*, saying *"surely they will reverence my*

Son." But when the Son came, those that possessed the vineyard said "*this is the heir, let us kill him and seize upon his inheritance.*"[47] This parable was prophetic of the most important issue of their time and ours: *the spirit of antichrist working through religious orthodoxy to steal the inheritance of God's Sons and Daughters.*

In the chapters that follow, we're going to look through God's loving, *jurisprudential eyes* and address the same issue that confronted Jesus of Nazareth at his trial in Jerusalem, namely: *What is **his relationship** with God and what does it mean to the rest of mankind?* We'll consider *his inheritance*, his *birthright*, and his *position* in Creation as the only ***begotten*** Son of God, and thereby determine our own position and inheritance in him, not only as *joint-heirs*, but also *as the **adopted** Sons and Daughters of God Almighty.* In order to do *justice* to these eternal questions, however, we will have to start at *the beginning*.

They that have ears to hear -- let them hear.

---

[47] Matthew 21:38, Mark 12:7, Luke 20:14.

CHAPTER ONE

The Beginning

AND SO IT IS WRITTEN, *"In the beginning God created the heavens and the earth. And the earth was without form and void, and darkness was on the face of the deep."[1]* The scriptures are careful to point out that the initial state of the earth was an empty, formless void; a thick gloomy darkness covering the face of the massive, lifeless oceans that spread across the planet. So even at the beginning, emptiness waited for a purpose, and for God to utter his voice.

Untold years later, the Apostle John would take us back to this very time – to the beginning -- to this shapeless, amorphous chaos that existed *before* the *Spirit of God moved* on the face of the waters, before God said, *"let there be light."* John would take us back to that place of eternal wisdom, where the *eternal purpose[2]* was

---

[1] Genesis 1:1-2

conceived *in God* -- before "evening and morning" would define the first day of creation.[3] *In the beginning was the Word*, John would tell us. This *Word* was the *eternal life and wisdom that was with the Father* then -- and that in time would be *manifest to us*.[4]

But here *before* the foundation of the world, *before* God said "let there be light," *before* God began to *form* his creation with his own breath, his own Spirit, and his own wisdom -- the scriptures tell us that *the earth was without form and void, darkness covering the face of the deep.* There was no shred of life, no spark of design, and no architecture to the prevailing *status quo* on the planet. Indeed, there was a notable *absence* of life and form. It was an inert, amorphous mass, covered in darkness. The truth is, before God spoke, the creation had as much life coursing through it as a lump of clay sitting on a motionless potter's wheel, ready to be formed, shaped, and molded by the artist. It is a remarkable picture; a murky corpus of water and earth, desolate and wholly dependent

---

[2] See, e.g., Ephesians 3:11 (*eternal purpose*), Romans 8:29 (*foreknown image*) I Corinthians 2:7 (*hidden wisdom*), Ephesians 1:5 (*predestined adoption*), II Timothy 1:9 (*purpose and grace given before the world began*); Titus 1:2 (*eternal life promised before the world*), I Peter 1:2 (*elect according to foreknowledge*), Revelation 13:8 (*book of life*).

[3] Genesis 1:5

[4] I John 1:2; See also, Proverbs 8:22-31(*wisdom personified*); I Corinthians 2:7 (*hidden wisdom ordained before the world*).

on God – that's the way it was, that's the way it all began, a wasteland, a black, primordial hollow.

Of course, it is no accident that the scene at the creation is set up this way; the contrast is intentional, strategically set up to make a powerful statement, the ultimate big picture -- a frame of reference none of us could miss. Even in darkness and emptiness, God was communicating with us, communicating with children not yet born and yet intimately *known* by name and yes, even in form.[5]

There can be no light or life without God, no form to the clay without the potter, and no finished vessel without a plan, purpose, and creative forethought or design.[6] This is what God was saying in the emptiness described in Genesis 1:1. As it is written of the *wisdom* of God that was with God from the beginning: *"The LORD possessed me in the beginning of his way, before his works of old. I was set up from everlasting, from the beginning or ever the earth was, when there were no depths I was brought forth."*[7]

The truth is, from the very foundation of the world the structure, form, and essence of life sprang from a Divine Plan *expressed* in time and space, an eternal

---

[5] Psalm 139:12-18; See also, Jeremiah 1:5; Revelation 13:8.

[6] Proverbs 8:22-31

[7] Proverbs 8:22-23

blueprint and architecture conceived in wisdom – and our Heavenly Father wanted us to know that. But more wonderful than that, even as darkness covered the face of the deep and chaos prevailed everywhere, this *hidden wisdom of God* was *ordained before the world to **our glory**.*[8] In other words, our spiritual *inheritance* was already *written* and *sealed* from the beginning.

THE ETERNAL SPIRIT

And the Spirit of God moved upon the face of the waters.[9] And so it began. Even as our lifeless planet was shrouded in gloom, the *eternal Spirit*[10] of God began to move, hover, and brood over the face of the roaring deep. It was a pregnant moment. The very instrumentality of God enveloped and prepared the desolate earth for a coming act of grace, love, design, and unspeakable beauty. The God who *inhabits eternity,*[11] who *sees the end from the beginning,*[12] the great *I AM*[13] was right there at that beginning, fully and *infinitely* comprehending each and every moment of what was to come, *beginning to end.*

---

[8] I Corinthians 2:7

[9] Genesis 1:2

[10] Hebrews 9:14 (*eternal Spirit*); See also, Deuteronomy 33:27 (*eternal God*).

[11] Isaiah 57:15

[12] Isaiah 46:10

[13] Exodus 3:14

"CAN ANY HIDE HIMSELF IN SECRET PLACES THAT I SHALL NOT SEE HIM, SAYS THE LORD. DO I NOT FILL HEAVEN AND EARTH SAYS THE LORD?"

JEREMIAH 23:24

This was a time of foreknowledge.[14] It was a time of mysteries[15] and of secrets known and knowable only to God and those to whom God would choose to reveal them.[16] It was a time when God's *eyes saw our substance*, when *all of our days were numbered*, and when *all of our members were written -- when as yet there was none of them*.[17] God already *knew* Jeremiah the prophet, had sanctified him, and had called him to his ministry.[18] God had already *chosen us* in the Messiah,[19] written each of our names in the *Lamb's Book of Life*,[20] and destined us to be conformed to *the **image** of his beloved Son*.[21] The God who *calls things that **are not** as though they were*[22] was

---

[14] Romans 11:2, Romans 8:29, Acts 2:23, I Peter 1:2, I Peter 1:20, Galatians 3:8.

[15] Mark 4:11, Romans 16:25, I Corinthians 15:51, Ephesians 1:9, 3:3, 3:4, 3:9, 5:32, 6:19, Revelation 10:7, I Timothy 3:16, Colossians 1:26, 2:2, 4:3.

[16] Deuteronomy 29:29, Judges 13:18, Proverbs 25:2, I Chronicles 28:9, Daniel 2:22, 12:9, Amos 3:7, I Corinthians 2:9-10, Mark 13:32, Romans 8:27, Job 11:7, Isaiah 40:28, Revelation 5:3, 10:4.

[17] Psalm 139:16

[18] Jeremiah 1:5

[19] Ephesians 1:4, II Thessalonians 2:13.

[20] Exodus 32:33, Daniel 12:1, Luke 10:20, Revelation 3:5, 13:8, 20:12, 21:27, 22:19.

[21] Romans 8:29

there, ready to speak of things *as if* they were finished, and from his *eternal point of view* they already were.[23] As David would one day exclaim, *"How precious also are your thoughts unto me O God! How great is the sum of them! If I should count them, they are more in number than the sand."*[24] Indeed, that was an understatement.

There is no darkness or unknowns in God, no obscurities, no blurred vistas in the distance, no hazy memories or vague ideas of what is to come. As it is written, *"...the darkness does not hide from you, but the night shines as the day; darkness and light are both alike to you."*[25] With God there is no *shadow of turning.*[26] God is without beginning or end, literally present at all times at once[27] -- omniscient, infinite, all-powerful, and Almighty. The only life in God is *eternal life.* So even before the world began, our *eternal* Father had already made the *promise* of eternal life[28] and was already standing at the finish line, waiting for *his children* to run into the stadium and receive their crown of glory and *inherit* the kingdom *prepared from the foundation of the world.*[29] The

---

[22] Romans 4:17, Acts 15:18.

[23] Hebrews 4:3

[24] Psalm 139:17-18

[25] Psalm 139:12

[26] James 1:17

[27] Deuteronomy 33:27; Hebrews 9:14, Isaiah 57:15.

[28] Titus 1:2

landscaping and precise bounty of God's *spiritual garden* was already foreknown in every detail before God uttered a single word. And then God spoke.

> "THROUGH FAITH WE UNDERSTAND THAT THE WORLDS
> WERE FRAMED BY THE WORD OF GOD, SO THAT THINGS WHICH ARE SEEN
> WERE NOT MADE OF THINGS WHICH DO APPEAR."
>
> HEBREWS 11:3

GOD'S LIGHT

"And God said, let there be light, and there was light."[30] Then, before the sun, before the moon, and even before the stars -- light suddenly appeared on the barren earth and bathed it in beauty. It was a profoundly meaningful sequence of events. The Apostle Paul would later record that God *commanded the light to shine out of darkness.*[31] The primordial abyss and formless void suddenly and profoundly changed. Darkness ran away; it was vanquished with the mere utterance of our Creator. The emptiness and void were filled and *definition* and *purpose* suddenly arose from the obscurity. The potter's wheel began to spin, and the potter's hands began to move with intent, care, and deliberation. It was as miraculous

---

[29] Matthew 25:34
[30] Genesis 1:3
[31] II Corinthians 4:6

and climactic as it was sovereign, measured, and thoughtful. With one utterance, one command, our dark and lifeless planet was suddenly and profoundly bathed in warm, nurturing, *light*.

We might imagine the earth at this time as basking in the grace and glory of God, just as the New Earth and New Jerusalem are described in the Book of Revelation, where it is written that *the city shall have no need of the sun, neither the moon to shine in it: for the glory of God did lighten it....*[32] Indeed, the *original* earth must have been a supernatural, even spiritual place. No sun, no moon, no stars – just the light of God.

God is Light, and in him is no darkness at all.[33] Angels, too, have an *innate* light to their being.[34] After spending time in the presence of God, the face of Moses shone so brightly with God's light and glory that he put a veil over his face when speaking to the children of Israel.[35] On the Mount of Transfiguration our Savior appeared in dazzling white light as he prayed,[36] and when the Apostle Paul encountered Messiah on the road to Damascus, Paul

---

[32] Revelation 21:23

[33] I John 1:5

[34] Judges 13:6, Revelation 10:1.

[35] Exodus 34:33-35, II Corinthians 3:13.

[36] Matthew 17:1-3

was literally blinded by the light of our Master's majesty and glory.[37]

According to the Genesis account, green grass, herbs, and fruit trees were all created *before* God created the sun, moon and stars.[38] This is because *light* itself is a much larger reality than what mere science can describe or even understand. Before matter and even before the laws of physics were *decreed* by the God who designed them and decided their application,[39] *there was light*. The scriptures tell us that Aaron's rod *budded* in the presence of God.[40] This is a precedent for a *spiritual* "photosynthesis," a plant-chemistry that transcends our natural understanding of science. As it is written also in the book of Isaiah, "*The sun shall be no more your light by day; neither for brightness shall the moon give you light: but the LORD shall be unto you an everlasting light, and your God, your glory.*"[41] The truth is, when God began to *speak* in Genesis, the universe was being *framed* with an unseen spiritual *Constitution of Light* – the Word of God. For with God -- nothing shall be impossible.[42]

---

[37] Acts 9:3-9

[38] Genesis 1:11-14

[39] Psalm 148:1-6, Nehemiah 9:6, Job 26:7, Hebrews 11:3.

[40] Numbers 17:1-8, Hebrews 9:4.

[41] Isaiah 60:19

[42] Luke 1:37

Of course, the *"seven days of creation"* outlined in the Book of Genesis are somewhat enigmatic and remain a mystery. They are undoubtedly set forth in symbolic and/or seed form, presenting a prophetic *spiritual outline* of things to come; but that being said, the account itself should not be taken as anything other than a wholly accurate record of events.[43]

So, for instance, it was *after* God said "let there be light," but *before* God made the sun, moon, and stars, that the scriptures tell us that *God divided the light from the darkness, calling the light "day," and the darkness "night."*[44] This was the *first day* of creation – a day literally without sunrise or sunset. God would only *later* create the sun and moon to *"rule day and night"* on earth in perpetuity.

And, not surprisingly, from this point forward *"day"* would be used as a metaphor to describe spiritual awareness and insight. Conversely, *"night"* would become a metaphor to describe spiritual darkness and blindness.[45] *Shadows*, both natural and spiritual,[46] were also a direct

---

[43] II Timothy 3:16, II Peter 1:19-21. *Note:* Whether the Genesis account is taken as allegorical, literal, or spiritual, every word of the account in the original text is inspired of God and authoritative as such.

[44] Genesis 1:4-5

[45] Deuteronomy 28:29, Micah 3:6, Matthew 6:23, 15:14, John 11:9-10; Romans 13:12, II Peter 1:19, Psalm 82:5.

[46] Song 2:17, Isaiah 32:2, 49:2, 51:16, Colossians 2:17, Hebrews 10:1, James

result of light, and the obstruction of that light. Interestingly, it wasn't until after the flood that God revealed the entire *spectrum* of light as a symbol or token of his *covenant* with Noah and all other living things to never again flood the earth.[47] In all this we see purpose, mystery, and sovereignty.

THE MYSTERY OF DESIGN

"...AND EVERY PLANT OF THE FIELD BEFORE IT WAS IN THE EARTH, AND EVERY HERB OF THE FIELD BEFORE IT GREW."

GENESIS 2:5

But even here in Genesis, God was *"calling things that **were not** as though **they were**."* As it is written, *"These are the generations of the heavens and the earth when they were created, in the day that the LORD God made the earth and the heavens, and every plant of the field **before it was in the earth**, and every herb of the field **before it grew**...."*[48] The truth is, God **made** every plant and herb of the field – **before** they grew. This is the mystery of design.

Because our Creator sees the end from the beginning, and **because** our Creator is also a designer, the *seeds of*

1:17.

[47] Genesis 9:8-17

[48] Genesis 2:4-5

life were in fact that life -- *in his eyes*. It could be no other way. The period of time between seed and flourishion would be *seen differently* from the perspective of an eternal, infinite being. The *reality* of life beginning and existing *as a seed* -- and the recognition *by God* of that seed as both *standing for* and *actually being* what it ultimately would become -- is innate to the story of Creation. *Every plant **before** it was in the earth, every herb **before** it grew* -- this is the mystery of our Father's Garden.

"I AM THE TRUE VINE,
AND MY FATHER IS THE GARDENER."

JOHN 15:1

How could the being who invented DNA, who invented seed, plant, and fruit -- not have planned, seen, and known *exactly* what diverse wonders would be "unpacked" from each of those blueprints, those seeds, and those designs -- even before he made them? It is the ultimate paradox of *the eternal purpose*. Creation itself *assumes* a profoundly detailed and complete forethought and advance-rendering in the intent, purpose, and being of the Creator. As it is written, *"He that planted the ear, shall he not hear? He that formed the eye, shall he not see?"*[49] The mere existence of a *seed* is evidence of *Divine* intent and purpose, for therein we find the *hidden architecture*, the intended sum and substance of what something is *meant* to be. As it is written:

*"For my **thoughts** are not your thoughts, neither are your ways my ways, Says the LORD. For as the heavens are higher than the earth, so are my ways higher than your ways, and my **thoughts** than your thoughts."*

"For as the rain comes down, and the snow from heaven, and returns not but waters the earth and makes it bring forth and bud, that it may give seed to the sower and bread to the eater:"

*"So shall my word be that goes forth from my mouth: it shall not return unto me void, but it shall accomplish that which I please, and it shall prosper **in that whereunto I sent it.**"*[50]

From the beginning, the intended and *eternal purpose* of God's infinite **forethought** was brought to pass *through* his spoken utterance, the *Word of Life*. This is the precise mystery of *design* and *existence*. And as we'll see, it is in **this** *mystery*, **this** *hidden wisdom ordained from the foundation of the world,* and **not** in the mere *span of time* **between** seed and fruit, that *Mankind* will discover his own *eternal purpose,* destiny, and inheritance.

---

[49] Psalm 94:9

[50] Isaiah 55:8-11

"BUT WE SPEAK THE WISDOM OF GOD IN A MYSTERY, EVEN THE HIDDEN WISDOM, WHICH GOD ORDAINED BEFORE THE WORLD UNTO OUR GLORY."

I CORINTHIANS 2:7

CHAPTER TWO

Mankind

"AND GOD SAID, LET US MAKE MAN IN OUR OWN IMAGE, AFTER OUR OWN LIKENESS: AND LET THEM HAVE DOMINION OVER THE FISH OF THE SEA, AND OVER THE FOWL OF THE AIR, AND OVER THE CATTLE, AND OVER ALL THE EARTH..."

GENESIS 1:26

AND SO THE STAGE was set for mankind before he finally appeared on the sixth day of creation.[1] Everything was good. Nothing was wrong. God's *sovereign utterance* or w*ord* framed the entirety of all that he made, forming the very *Constitution* of all things spiritual and physical, heavenly and earthly, from beginning to end, from the subatomic to the outermost reaches of space, time, and dimension.[2] God planted a vast and beautiful garden, called it *"Eden"* or *"Paradise,"* and God anticipated *mankind* would tend it and keep it as a home, as an environment, as a nurturing place of abode.[3] At some point on this timeline God also created an innumerable company of angels,[4] spirit-beings

---

[1] Genesis 1:24-31
[2] Hebrews 11:3
[3] Genesis 2:15
[4] Hebrews 12:22. *Note*: Because the serpent, who we know was Satan (Revelation

designed *to minister* to and for man on God's behalf.[5] And so it is written that when all of God's work was finished, God was pleased, and on the seventh day the infinite, eternal, omniscient God of all Creation *rested*.[6]

MAN'S DOMINION

In creating mankind, God designed and minted him in his own *image and likeness*;[7] God then formed the *first man* Adam from the dust of the earth.[8] Man was given nobility, made God's offspring, God's child, God's sons and daughters, God's representative vessel -- even a holy *tabernacle* for God's *indwelling by his Spirit*.[9] This role in the creation was an unspeakable and profound honor that man was designed to comprehend, enjoy, and explore over time.

In giving man life, God imparted his own breath[10] and Spirit into man's innermost being, allowing man to partake of and share in God's very essence, nature, and character

---

12:9), was listed as the most subtle (Genesis 3:1) of the *"beasts of the field"* created on the sixth day (Genesis 1:24-25), we might conclude that all of the angels were created by God on the sixth day of the Genesis account.

[5] Hebrews 1:14

[6] Genesis 2:2

[7] Genesis 1:26

[8] Genesis 2:7

[9] I Corinthians 3:16, 6:19, II Corinthians 6:16, Ephesians 2:20-22, I Peter 2:5.

[10] Genesis 2:7

within. This furthered God's *intent and promise* that man would bear his image and likeness. God also put a *"Tree of Life"* in the midst of the garden,[11] a tree whose fruit and very existence bore *the promise* to forever extend the life that God had already imparted. God also planted the *Tree of the Knowledge of Good and Evil* in the Garden of Eden,[12] which, as we'll see, presented mankind with a meaningful and profound choice as he exercised the *free will* that came with his nobility.

In establishing man on the earth, God gave man dominion, position, and stewardship over *everything he had made* -- over the Garden of Eden, the earth, and over every other physical, natural, and spiritual thing that God had created.[13] While the angels were *gifted* with supernatural abilities to exercise in their role as ministering spirits,[14] man's original relationship to God as his *"Sons and Daughters"* put him in authority and dominion over the angels as well.[15] The basis of this dominion, however, was explicitly rooted in man's *continuing relationship* with the Creator.

---

[11] Genesis 2:9

[12] Id.

[13] Genesis 1:28, Psalm 8:6, 82:6.

[14] Hebrews 1:14

[15] Hebrews 2:5-9, Psalm 8:3-8.

Even so, all of what was granted and delivered to mankind from the beginning was irrevocably ordained by God for his children, for his *Sons and Daughters*. It was mankind's birthright, an *inheritance* from a *loving and just* Heavenly Father. This gave us accountability, ownership, jurisdiction, and a deep sense of nobility and dignity we could enjoy for eternity.

THE REBELLION

But something happened on the road to that eternity. Something disrupted the goodness of God's universe, derailing the calling, purpose, and position God had established and ordained for man *from the beginning.* Man's Sonship, his relationship to God *as child of God and therefore **heir** of God,*[16] was lost, and his nobility surrendered. The *accountability* that came with mankind's noble position in creation now gave way to *responsibility* for man's open and willful disobedience to the God who created him.[17]

Sin entered the once perfect creation, and darkness, emptiness, and disorder soon threatened man's very existence. Death, murder, violence, greed, disease, war,

---

[16] Romans 8:17, Galatians 4:7, Titus 3:7, Hebrews 1:14, Hebrews 6:17.
[17] Genesis 2:16-17, 3:19, Proverbs 11:19, Ezekiel 18:4, Romans 5:12, 6:23.

starvation, rebellion, crime, punishment, hurt, sorrow, and tears soon invaded the earth, and wouldn't let it go. "Weeds, thorns, and thistles" invaded the ground man was taken from,[18] and delusions of grandeur and *blinding* self-interest invaded the mind and heart of God's, once noble children.

Rather than remain the glorious and vividly beautiful *spiritual and organic* environment where God would nurture and care for his increasingly enlightened children, the earth instead became a *breeding ground* for organized resistance against the values and interests of its Creator. God's character became unpalatable to the *fallen tastes* of a suddenly self-centered humanity. The value of an *eternal* relationship with a Father and God who loved and provided was rejected in favor of other, more *temporal* desires, desires that seemed to appear out of nowhere as man's heart brought forth the fruit of a newly found state of emptiness, vanity, and self-will.[19]

Contrary to God's commandment, man partook of the *Tree of the Knowledge of Good and Evil.* Man made a choice he was free to make, but it was the wrong choice. And, as God had promised,[20] man died *spiritually* on the

---

[18] Genesis 3:17-19

[19] Ecclesiastes 9:3, Jeremiah 17:9, Mark 7:21.

[20] Genesis 2:17

very day he disobeyed his Creator, and that spiritual death ultimately led to his physical death as well.[21] Eternity and Paradise were lost. The scarcity of life -- death itself -- now set a *new price* on everything in man's world, chasing up the value of all things temporal. Mankind's *values* would thereafter change dramatically as he desperately clung to the perceived *finiteness* of his own existence.

As time unfolded thereafter, a world of temporal distractions and causes sprang up over the face of man's fallen realm. Man's "world" became an arcade for him to play in, a stadium for his games, a market for his trade, a battlefield for his wars, and a forum for his endless captivation to self-fulfillment and temporal pleasure.[22] This new world, this order, this array, with all its cosmetic[23] and carnal appeal, soon seized control of man's hours, days, weeks, months, years, and life-span. The *fashion of this world*, though as transitory as a vapor[24] and just as meaningless, now became the object of sacrifice for its devoted fans. Over time, kingdoms rose and fell. Armies marched, and were marched upon. Cities were sacked, rebuilt, and then sacked again. But the values and dreams

---

[21] I Corinthians 15:21-23

[22] I John 2:15-17, James 4:4, Ephesians 2:2, II Timothy 4:10, James 1:10-11.

[23] *Note:* The word "world" comes from the word "cosmos," from which we derive the idea of "cosmetic."

[24] I Corinthians 7:31

of fallen humanity endured without interruption, being the plunder of each successive conqueror, and the inheritance of each successive generation. The actors changed, but the play stayed the same.

THE ADVERSARY

And yet, something even more insidious and troubling lay at the heart of mankind's plunge into darkness and decomposition over the ages. Something else was happening behind the scenes, something invisible to the eye but evident as the world took shape over time and as each generation followed a blueprint secretly and deceptively laid out in their fallen hearts and souls from birth.

Unbeknownst to mankind, his entire world-view had been taken captive, imprisoned, and made the servant of a powerful and innately gifted *fallen angel* whom God had created with extraordinary ability and beauty,[25] a being who's true agenda was his own enthronement as king, and as the deity of man's civilization.[26] The serpent,[27] Satan, a spirit-being or *cherub* initially created to be a public

---

[25] Genesis 3:1, Ezekiel 28:11-15.
[26] Luke 4:6, I Corinthians 4:4, II Thessalonians 2:9, Matthew 13:38-38, John 12:31, 14:30, 16:11, Revelation 13:1-6.
[27] Revelation 12:9

servant of the highest order,[28] decided instead that the earth should be *his planet*, and that mankind should be enlisted in his ultimate causes, to serve his ultimate ends.

Rebelling against God's *eternal purpose and wisdom* for mankind, Satan led vast numbers of angels, spirit beings of every rank, order, and type, and arrayed them in formal opposition to mankind's place in creation. Man sinned, and *angels fell* into the vacuum created by man's loss of dominion, now lured by the opportunity to seize man's inheritance. Satan thus became *the prince of this new world order,*[29] and he began to *traffic*[30] in the acquisition of power, influence, and world domination.[31]

It was pride that caused Satan's fall.[32] A fire burned within him. He wanted to rule, to be acknowledged, to have centre-stage, to be exalted, praised, and recognized for who and what he was. He was captivated by his own splendor and God-given position.[33] In his own eyes, the grandness of his *innate ability* cried out for expression, fulfillment, and an overwhelming need for closure. He could not rest until every *dimension* of man's dominion,

---

[28] Ezekiel 28:14

[29] John 14:30

[30] Ezekiel 28:18

[31] II Corinthians 4:4, Luke 4:6, Revelation 13:1-6.

[32] Ezekiel 28:17

[33] Id.

until every aspect of man's initial grant of authority at creation, until all of man's *inheritance* was fully surrendered to his spiritual, ideological, and *legal* control and influence.[34] Man's birthright was for sale, and Satan was a motivated buyer.

The fall of man in the Garden of Eden put the rights to the cosmetic, temporal, superficial, and material fallen world in Satan's power, and he savoured[35] the opportunity to be its designer and architect as he used that world, *and the death that had created it*, to dominate man spiritually. Working through unseen principalities and powers in the heavenly realm,[36] as well as through demonic foot soldiers on earth,[37] Satan would work to build a kingdom of his own design, and in his own image[38] -- and in time billions of beings would whistle his fallen angelic tunes as they worked on behalf of his fallen angelic causes. *"All the kingdoms of this world and the glory of them"* became his possession, and his property -- to deal with as he saw fit.[39] All he needed was investors, and they blindly lined up in droves.

---

[34] Revelation 12:10, II Corinthians 4:4.

[35] Matthew 16:23, Mark 8:33

[36] Ephesians 6:12

[37] Matthew 8:29, Mark 1:4, 3:11, Luke 4:41, Acts 19:15.

[38] Revelation 13:15

[39] Luke 4:6

THE REMNANT

Not all was lost, however. Not all was lost. For in comparison to the vast expanse of eternity that our Heavenly Father *inhabited* and that he had, from the beginning, *irrevocably* promised to share with his *children*, Satan's reign was *destined* to be as short-lived and temporal as the world he so lusted to dominate. After generations in the building and just as it would reach its apparent zenith,[40] Satan's kingdom would have an end, and in *justice and fairness*, that end would come at the hand of the very *humanity* that he had sought to enlist in his self-centered cause. For even as the vast majority[41] of the world occupied itself with the dream of building a *great city* or *kingdom* on earth whose builder and maker was Satan,[42] a small but mighty remnant[43] of mankind would fill their hearts with the vision of occupying an eternal city and kingdom from heaven, whose builder and maker was God.[44]

Even from the beginning,[45] some of mankind would trust not in themselves,[46] but *separate themselves* from the

---

[40] Revelation 13:7

[41] Matthew 7:13-14

[42] Genesis 11:1-6, Revelation 13:7-8, 17:1-18, 18:1-24.

[43] Isaiah 1:9, Jeremiah 23:3, Romans 9:27, 11:5.

[44] Hebrews 11:10, 13-16.

[45] Genesis 4:4

self-centered masses and seek deliverance from a world whose destiny of destruction had already been *written and sealed by the Judge of all the Earth*. A remnant of humanity would not be fooled by the glitter and glamour of fallen man's inventions, by the loftiness of fallen man's dreams, or by the attractions and fashions of fallen man's selfish and temporal world. A small remnant would refuse to invest their hours, days, weeks and life-spans in an account that would turn up empty at the end of the day. A small remnant would pierce through the darkness of each successive age of history, see the promise of eternity through the eyes of faith, and thereby lay hold on their *eternal inheritance,* an inheritance that would render the past, present, and future of fallen humanity, with all its hopes, dreams, values, and delusions of grandeur, a mere speck on the mural of forever.

This *resistance*[47] would ultimately be led by a *promised seed* of *the woman*[48] Eve, a new and sinless Adam[49] *foreknown* and *foreordained* from the beginning[50]

---

[46] *Note:* This distinction is seen in the story of Cain and Abel (Genesis 4:1-16). Cain offered God the works of his own hands, while Abel offered God of the work of God's hands. It was a teachable moment, and also a reflection of what was in each man's heart.

[47] Revelation 2:7, 2:17, 2:26, 3:5, 3:12, 21, 12:11.

[48] Genesis 3:15

[49] I Corinthians 15:45-47

[50] I Peter 1:19-20

and *hidden in God* as the very wisdom and purpose of all that God would do for his children.[51] This *second Adam*[52] would be sent from heaven at *the end of time* to redeem his brethren[53] from the grip of Satan, sin, and death. But in order to do so he would have to endure, overcome, suffer, and die.

He would be called *The Messiah*.

---

[51] Colossians 1:16
[52] I Corinthians 15:47
[53] Hebrews 2:11

CHAPTER THREE

The Messiah

O N THE NIGHT of his betrayal, after the Last Supper, after showing his disciples with the symbols of bread and wine how best to remember him and what he was about to do, Jesus of Nazareth, the Galilean Jew and teacher who would have been known by his Hebrew name *Yeshua*, was drawn into prayer, and into a spiritual battlefield that few have understood. It was his hour of trial, his hour of temptation, an hour that would last all night and into the morning until he was completely *emptied*,[1] until everything he was and everything he had was fully and irrevocably surrendered to the will of his Father, and his God.[2] It was a night that would begin in prayer, and end in trial, scourging, crucifixion, and death. But he made his *purpose* clear as he led his disciples into the darkest night in human history.

---

[1] Isaiah 53:12, Philippians 2:7
[2] Revelation 3:12

*"That the world may know that **I love the Father**...."*[3] It was that love, therefore, the love of Yeshua for his Heavenly Father, which would fuel and define *his Passion.*

THE PRINCE OF THIS WORLD

It would begin in a garden. Yeshua took his disciples to a place called *Gethsemane,*[4] a secluded wooded area on the Mount of Olives where he had often prayed when in Jerusalem. He was distant, not speaking much with them. He had told them a little about what was to come, but not much. *"Hereafter I will not speak much with you"* he told them, *"for the prince of this world comes, and has nothing in me."*[5] This revealed that a spiritual battle with Satan stood between him and the cross, and between a *sinless* life and an *undeserved* death. But as the prophet Isaiah had foretold, our Savior's *face was set like flint*[6] to fulfill his calling, and there was no turning back in the heart of this, the only *begotten.*[7]

---

3 John 14:31
4 Matthew 26:36
5 John 14:30. *See also,* Ephesians 4:27 (Neither give place to the devil).
6 Isaiah 50:7
7 John 3:16, Hebrews 1:5.

"HE IS NEAR WHO JUSTIFIES ME; WHO WILL CONTEND WITH ME? LET US STAND TOGETHER. WHO IS MY ADVERSARY? LET HIM COME NEAR ME."

ISAIAH 50:8

Of course, the *Messiah* and *Prophet*[8] who generations thereafter would call *Christ* had contended with *the prince of this world* before. At the very beginning of his ministry just a few years earlier, *Rabbi*[9] *Yeshua* had been *driven by the Spirit into the wilderness*[10] to undergo a carefully crafted sequence of *temptations* at the hands of the very *serpent*[11] who had successfully engineered the "fall of man" in *the Garden of Eden*.[12] The wilderness ordeal had been grueling, but in the end *empowering*.[13]

Forty days and forty nights Yeshua was without food or water, praying alone, exposed to the elements, and with the *wild beasts*.[14] But even weakened and weary in the flesh and close to death, the *one* John the Baptist would call *"The Lamb of God"*[15] had *overcome*[16] that trial without a single miss-step, standing against all temptation

---

[8] Luke 7:16, 13:33, 24:19, Mark 6:4, Acts 3:22, 7:37.
[9] Matthew 23:7-8, John 1:38, 49, 3:2, 26, 6:26 (*Note*: "Rabbi" means "Master").
[10] Mark 1:12
[11] Revelation 12:9
[12] Genesis 3
[13] Luke 14:4
[14] Mark 1:13
[15] John 1:29
[16] Revelation 3:21

by *trusting* in his Father's Word, and his Father's Word alone. *"If you are the Son of God"* the devil taunted, trying to lure Yeshua into proving who he was.[17] But Yeshua had come, not to prove himself, but to *empty himself.*[18] He would have none of it, despite the obvious contradiction presented as Satan showed him *"all the kingdoms of this world, and their glory,"* and then offered *all of it* to him.[19] But our Savior had come, not to accept offers *from the god of this world,*[20] but rather to remove Satan's dominion[21] and destroy his works.[22] So the Son of God took up *the Sword of the Spirit*[23] and resisted.[24]

"It is written," said our great and eternal *High Priest,*[25] the *Apostle* of our profession[26] who was *made perfect through sufferings.*[27] *"It is written,"* said the *author and finisher of faith*[28] who is now our *heavenly advocate with the Father*[29] and the *only mediator between God and man.*[30]

---

[17] Luke 4:3, 9

[18] Isaiah 53:12, Philippians 2:4-8.

[19] Luke 4:6

[20] II Corinthians 4:4

[21] Hebrews 2:5-14

[22] I John 3:8

[23] Ephesians 6:17

[24] James 4:7, I Peter 5:9,

[25] Hebrews 5:5-6, 10, 8:1-9:28

[26] Hebrews 3:1

[27] Hebrews 2:10, 5:8

[28] Hebrews 12:2

[29] I John 2:1

"It is written," said our *Good Shepherd,*[31] the *Son of Man,*[32] *the Pattern Son,*[33] *the Light of the World,*[34] and *Last Adam*[35] whose *example*[36] of service, loyalty, and *humility*[37] would thereafter define *the way, the truth, and the life*[38] for millions of *his brethren*[39] to follow. The *Anointed* of God[40] stood his ground in the wilderness, living *every moment* as he taught others to live – by *every word* that proceeds out of the mouth of God.[41]

A NIGHT IN PRAYER

But as Yeshua *prepared his heart* and *soul* on the eve of this, his final battle in Gethsemane, the Bible records that our loving Savior *began to be sorrowful, and deeply distressed.*[42] This night in prayer was going to be different, the depth of the struggle more demanding, the test of devotion and sacrifice more piercing and penetrating. In

---

[30] II Timothy 2:5

[31] John 10:11

[32] Matthew 9:6, Matthew 12:8.

[33] II Peter 2:21

[34] John 8:12

[35] I Corinthians 15:45

[36] John 13:15

[37] Zechariah 9:9, Matthew 11:29, John 13:5.

[38] John 14:6

[39] Hebrews 2:11

[40] Luke 4:18, Isaiah 61:1.

[41] Deuteronomy 8:3, Job 23:12, Psalm 119:103, Jeremiah 15:16, Matthew 4:4.

[42] Matthew 26:37

fact, in the very midst of it all Yeshua told his disciples that *his soul* was so burdened with anguish that he sensed his very life slipping away from him: "*My soul is exceedingly sorrowful, even unto death,*" he told them.[43] At one point our Messiah even asked his closest disciples to pray with him.[44] Then, going a stone's throw beyond them, the Bible tells us that Yeshua *prayed even more earnestly,*[45] no doubt for an extended period because he would later return to find his disciples had *fallen asleep.* On this night angels would be sent to *strengthen* him;[46] but here, alone, God's only begotten Son fell on his face and sought *the face* of his Father.

Yeshua of Nazareth was no stranger to prayer. It was not uncommon for him to go out alone to a solitary place and pray through the night and into the morning.[47] We might imagine the "prayer life" of *the beloved Son,*[48] the man who *dwelt in* the Father's bosom,[49] the only man who truly *knew* the Father intimately.[50] The scriptures provide a

---

[43] Matthew 26:38

[44] Id. *Note:* Peter, James, and John are commonly referred to as Messiah's "inner circle" of disciples. They alone were taken when Jesus healed the ruler of the synagogue's (Jairus) daughter (Mark 5:35-43), and to the Mount of Transfiguration (Mark 9:2-10).

[45] Luke 22:44

[46] Luke 22:43

[47] Matthew 14:23, Mark 1:35; 6:46, Luke 5:16; 6:12; 9:18.

[48] Matthew 3:17, 12:18, Ephesians 1:6, Colossians 1:13, II Peter 1:17.

[49] John 1:18

rich record of the heavenly visions and experiences that prophets and other men of God had during their time alone with God. Moses had asked to see God's glory[51]and the record of his experience and reflection of God's glory is forever with us.[52] The prophet Ezekiel had been *caught away in the Spirit* on a number of occasions, the *heavens being opened* to him.[53] At such times Ezekiel beheld wonders fantastic in their dimensions. Daniel, Zechariah, and others experienced visitations of angels, messengers of God who would often manifest the very presence of God himself.[54] The Apostle John would pen the entire book of Revelation based on a profound and lengthy vision of the spirit-realm. The Apostle Paul once testified that his visions and experiences in the Spirit were so incredible that a messenger of Satan was allowed to buffet him -- lest he become too *lifted up in pride* because of what he had seen.[55]

So of course Messiah Yeshua's own familiarity with the Spirit-realm must have been extraordinarily profound. At his baptism in the river Jordan it is written that the

---

[50] Exodus 33:20, Matthew 11:27, John 5:37; 6:46.

[51] Exodus 33:18

[52] Exodus 33:17-34:35, II Corinthians 3:7-15.

[53] Ezekiel 1:1-11:25

[54] Exodus 3:2, Isaiah 63:9, Acts 7:30, 35-38.

[55] II Corinthians 12:1-9

heavens were *opened unto him*.[56] Those heavens would not close until Messiah hung on the cross. While Moses was denied a *face-to-face* meeting with our Heavenly Father,[57] God's *only begotten Son* would have had such a meeting, and more.[58] Yeshua told a disciple named Nathaniel that he would see the *angels of God ascending and descending* upon the Son of man.[59] This was a reference to a *heavenly vision* Jacob once had at a place he would call the *house of God*.[60] Jacob could not have known then how prophetic and revelatory that experience would turn out to be for generations to follow.

JACOB'S LADDER

Jacob, the man who would become *Israel*[61] had camped out under the stars after a long journey from Beersheba to Haran. He had found a stone to use as a head-rest and he fell asleep. In a dream that night Jacob saw *a ladder set up on the earth, the top of which reached into heaven, and the angels of God ascending and descending upon it*.[62] Above it stood the LORD, who

---

[56] Matthew 3:16
[57] Exodus 33:19-23
[58] John 6:46, Matthew 18:10.
[59] John 1:51
[60] *Bethel* (Genesis 28:19)
[61] Genesis 32:28

spoke at length to Jacob saying, *"I am the LORD God of Abraham your father, and the God of Isaac: the land whereon you lay I will give to you and your seed and your seed will be as the dust of the earth. And you shall spread abroad to the west and to the east and to the north and to the south, and in you shall all the families of the earth be blessed. And, behold, I am with you and will keep you in all places wherever you go, and will bring you again to this land; for I will not leave you until I have done that which I have spoken to you."*[63]

When Jacob arose from this dream he understood that it was a message from God and that the place where he was, and where he had rested his head, was spiritually significant. *"This is none other than the house of God,"* Jacob exclaimed. *"This is the gate of heaven!"*[64] When Jacob got up the following morning he took *the stone* he had used as a pillow and stood it upright, pouring anointing oil on the top of it. He then made a vow unto *the God of Israel*, saying, *"If God will be with me, and will keep me in this way that I go, and will give me bread to eat, and clothes to put on, so that I come again to my father's house, then shall the LORD be my God, and this*

---

[62] Genesis 28:11-19
[63] Genesis 28:13-15
[64] Genesis 28:17

*stone which I have set for a pillar shall be **God's house**...*"[65]

An anointed stone, the house of God, and a ladder reaching into heaven: all of this was prophetic of Yeshua of Nazareth.[66] As it is written, *"For there is one God, and one **mediator between** God and man, **the man** Christ Jesus."*[67]

So yes, as the one *who bridged heaven and earth,* God's only begotten Son undoubtedly had an intimate prayer life. Yeshua was immersed in and filled with the Spirit[68] of his Father. Our Messiah's own description of prayer was revealing of the way he thought about it: *"When you pray, enter into your closet, and when you have shut your door, pray to your Father which is in secret; and your Father which sees in secret will reward you openly."*[69] Yeshua would have understood the *secret place of the Most High*[70] better than anyone.[71] For Yeshua of Nazareth, his closet of prayer was a place of spiritual intimacy, a place of relationship and fellowship that none had ever known.

---

[65] Genesis 28:20-22

[66] John 3:34, John 14:10, Colossians 1:19; 2:9.

[67] I Timothy 2:5

[68] John 3:12-13, 34

[69] Matthew 6:5

[70] Psalm 91:1

[71] John 14:10-11, 20, 15:10.

MAN OF SORROWS

"HE IS DESPISED AND REJECTED OF MEN; A MAN OF SORROWS AND AQUANTED WITH GRIEF…"

ISAIAH 53:3

But as he prayed in the *Garden of Gethsemane* on the eve of his crucifixion and death, the Gospel of Luke records that Messiah Yeshua's *secret place* now became a place of the deepest anguish and sorrow. Our Savior became so pressed, so heavy with the burden he was carrying, that the sweat on his face became "*as great drops of blood, falling to the ground.*"[72] His closet of prayer and intimacy with his Heavenly Father would now define his struggle. The truth is our Savior wrestled in the depths of his own heart. Yeshua fought and contended, grappling with his own call to *absolute obedience*[73] and the *perfection through suffering*[74] that his *own* Father had set before him in the final hours of his life on earth. Our Master's *character and identity* were being *tested and tried in the white-hot furnace* of what his *own Father* was asking him to accept and endure.

---

[72] Luke 22:44
[73] Hebrews 5:8
[74] Hebrews 2:10

Yeshua would later testify that if he asked, his Father would send more than *twelve legions of angels* to rescue him from what was coming that night and morning.[75] But this *servant of God*[76] also knew that *from the beginning* it had been his Father's *will* to *bruise* him, and to make *his soul* an *offering* for the sins of *the world God so loved.*[77] And, as he had told his disciples that very night, Yeshua wanted that world to **know** *that he loved the Father.*[78] So our Savior continued to pray, to contend, to fight, and to allow the sword[79] of his Father's Spirit to pierce to the very bone and marrow of who he was.[80]

"AWAKE, O SWORD, AGAINST MY SHEPHERD, AGAINST THE MAN WHO IS MY COMPANION, SAYS THE LORD OF HOSTS. STRIKE THE SHEPHERD, AND THE SHEEP WILL BE SCATTERED..."

ZECHARIAH 13:7

We can hardly imagine our beloved Savior's challenge that night. On three occasions during this time of agony and intercession in the *Garden of Gethsemane* Yeshua prayed for the possibility of another way, another remedy, another answer than the one put before him,

---

[75] Matthew 26:53

[76] Isaiah 42:1

[77] Genesis 3:15, Isaiah 53:10-12.

[78] John 14:31

[79] Hebrews 4:12

[80] Hebrews 4:13

saying: "*O My*[81] *Father, if it is possible, let this cup pass from me.*" But *the beloved* would also include an important bottom line which has come to characterize true *discipleship* for all who would follow in his footsteps: "N*evertheless, not as I will, but your will be done.*"[82]

Of course, Yeshua was facing more than what is commonly understood as death, more than trial and false accusation, more than humiliation and scourging, and even more than the unique challenge of having to endure it all without slipping, without sin, without flinching even once as the pressures of each moment mounted. Indeed, though other men have endured crucifixion, no other man has ever been asked to endure such a fate without allowing feelings of ill-will, un-forgiveness, self-pity, bitterness, resentment, anger, doubt, or unbelief to take root within -- let alone to endure it all with an abiding *sacrificial love* for each of his accusers and persecutors.[83]

But this calling was part of the *price* of our redemption. Yeshua's mission was to present himself as a *spotless* lamb, a *holy* offering and sacrifice in fulfillment of an *eternal purpose*, a calling to literal perfection of character and life made possible by the most difficult of

---

[81] Mark 14:36 "*Abba, Father.*"
[82] Luke 22:42, John 3:16.
[83] Isaiah 53:12, Luke 22:32, Matthew 5:43-48.

trials and tests -- and then to accept the *infinite injustice* of a death that would end that *perfect*, holy life.[84]

> **"SURELY HE HAS BORNE OUR GRIEFS, AND CARRIED OUR SORROWS: YET WE DID ESTEEM HIM STRICKEN, SMITTEN OF GOD AND AFFLICTED."**
>
> ISAIAH 53:4

Indeed, many people have been tortured and killed in human history. But not a single one of them has ever faced it under a continuing *requirement* of absolute and unwavering *perfection* in attitude, conduct, and thought. And if this were not enough, certainly no other has ever faced such an ordeal *knowing* the entire time that he could escape it all with one, simple request. Twelve legions of angels stood ready to move if Yeshua made the petition.

We might ask ourselves about *the depth* of such a calling and sacrifice, and the *beauty of the soul* who said *yes* to his Father at every turn, resisting all *temptation* to do otherwise. This Galilean Jew of the first century whose literal, biological Father[85] was the Creator himself, would not only have to endure the trial, torture, and humiliation of what was to come *without sinning in his heart* -- but he

---

[84] *Note*: Yeshua's suffering and crucifixion was an "infinite injustice" because Yeshua was sinless, harmless, holy, and infinitely noble as the only begotten Son of God.

[85] Luke 1:31, 35

would have to endure it all while having the continuing *option* of being *rescued* from it at any time.

And yet, most would agree that when all the elements of what Yeshua of Nazareth was facing in the *Garden of Gethsemane* that night are considered together, the *"cup"* that he was being asked to drink involved more than the trial and torture, more than the challenge of remaining *pure in heart* and *without sin* through it all, and more than the temptation to call for angels. There was something much deeper going on in Yeshua's heart as he prayed; something *beyond the veil* of physical suffering and death. Yeshua was being asked to *surrender* his greatest treasure -- his own pearl of great price – *the relationship* he had with *his God.*

"MY GOD, MY GOD,
WHY HAST THOU FORSAKEN ME?"

PSALM 22:1

CHAPTER FOUR

Beyond the Veil

AT THE CORE of Yeshua's final test in the *Garden of Gethsemane* was the Holy Place, his Father's Temple, the secret place of the Most High, the place of *God's dwelling*, God's Holy Tabernacle – that *place within Yeshua* himself where his Father's *glory and presence* had found a home, at long last, in man.[1] Yeshua of Nazareth was facing an impending *separation* from his Father, the loss of spiritual and personal *union* with his God, the loss of *the relationship* that *defined him* and that he had *abided in* and enjoyed every day of his life. *"He who knew no sin"* was literally being asked to *become sin*[2] on the cross, and that meant he would have to endure, *personally*, the infinite separation[3] that exists between darkness and light, between the absolute *holiness*

---

[1] John 3:34
[2] II Corinthians 5:21
[3] Isaiah 59:2, 64:7.

of a just God and the absolute depravity and *emptiness* of fallen man without God.

It was this *Holy Place*, this living, experiential, vivid, *fruit-bearing* reality of the *continuing and abiding* presence of his Father *within him* that Yeshua was **also** being asked to surrender that night in the garden, and the value and meaning of that *treasure* to Yeshua's pure heart and soul cannot be quantified. Yeshua was the literal *Temple of God* on earth.[4] He had never known a single moment in his life separated from his God and Father. He lived with his Father *within him*, and *within* him in his absolute *fullness*.[5] Now Yeshua was being asked to endure the abandonment of his *Father's Spirit* from that Holy Place, that place *beyond the veil*, that place reserved and *designed* for the glory of God -- and no scourge or nail could come close to inflicting that kind of personal agony, anguish, and suffering.

---

[4] John 2:19-21
[5] Colossians 1:19, 2:9, John 3:34.

THE ANOINTED ONE

Yeshua was unique. He had testified that he could do *nothing of himself*,[6] and that he *abided* in the Father and the Father *abided* in him.[7] He and his Father *were one*.[8] As stated above, the Apostle John described Yeshua as someone whose natural *abode,* his spiritual home, was *"in the bosom of the Father."*[9] This intimacy and *oneness* with the Father was all our Master had ever known. John the Baptist would testify that Yeshua had the Spirit *without measure,*[10] an essentially unlimited *anointing*.

In fact, the word *"Messiah"* (Hebrew) and the word *"Christ"* (Greek) both mean *"anointed one,"* speaking literally of *the oil of anointing that designated a prophet as a representative of God*, but symbolically of the very *Spirit of God* upon and *within* a *chosen vessel* of God's service. In this case the vessel's anointing was boundless, and his representative capacity perfect, full, and *seamless*. Yeshua and his Father were *one* via his *Sonship*[11] and the

---

[6] John 5:19, 30

[7] John 14:9-11

[8] John 10:30. *Note:* Yeshua explained his *oneness* with the Father when he prayed in John 17:21-22: *"That they all may be one; as you, Father, are in me, and I in you, that they also may be one is us; that the world may believe that you have sent me. And the glory which you gave me I have given them; that they may be one, even as we are one."*

[9] John 1:18

[10] John 3:34

limitless anointing that would ultimately[12] accompany that Sonship. As John the Baptist testified just after referring to Yeshua's profound, unlimited anointing, *"The Father loves the Son, and has given all things into his hand."*[13] That's who Yeshua was, the *anointed one, the Son of God* anointed *without measure* with the *oil of gladness.*[14]

> "THERE SHALL COME FORTH A ROD FROM THE STEM OF JESSE, AND A BRANCH SHALL GROW OUT OF HIS ROOTS. THE SPIRIT OF THE LORD SHALL REST UPON HIM, THE SPIRIT OF WISDOM AND UNDERSTANDING, THE SPIRIT OF COUNSEL AND MIGHT, THE SPIRIT OF KNOWLEDGE AND OF THE FEAR OF THE LORD."
>
> ISAIAH 11:1-2

It is certainly no coincidence, then, that the word *"Gethsemane"* literally means *"oil press;"* and this meaning could not have been lost on Yeshua of Nazareth that night as he prayed. For there in the *Oil Press of God*, there in the *Garden of Gethsemane*, God's *Anointed* was being asked to willingly endure an event that would *press* the very *oil* of his *existence*, the oil *of his life*, the

---

[11] *Note:* In John 10:30, Yeshua testified that he and his Father were one. When the Jews picked up stones to stone him for "blasphemy" Yeshua replied *"why do you call it blasphemy if I say I am the Son of God?"*

[12] *Note:* When Yeshua came out of the waters of John's baptism, it is written that the Spirit descended from heaven like a dove and abode and remained upon him. It was in seeing that event that John the Baptist *"bore record"* that Yeshua was *"the Son of God"* (John 1:32-34).

[13] John 3:35

[14] Hebrews 1:9, Psalm 45:7.

anointing that defined him and made him who and what he was, the very *Spirit* that filled him – completely out of his human frame, leaving *his soul* alone and without the life-blood of *his spiritual being*. This "death" none of us can imagine.

THE LAMB OF GOD

"BEHOLD THE LAMB OF GOD WHO TAKES AWAY THE SIN OF THE WORLD."

JOHN 1:29

Yeshua was intimately familiar with all the *Messianic* prophecies, from God's pronouncement in Genesis that *the seed of the woman* would be bruised by the serpent,[15] to John the Baptist's identification of him as the *Son of God* and the *Lamb of God*.[16] Our Messiah always understood what his calling was. Yeshua had observed many Passovers and had been to Jerusalem yearly since childhood, there to watch the sacrificial lambs carried into the Temple to go to their death. He knew, he always knew, who and what those lambs really pointed to. He knew *who* they pre-figured, and *why* they were giving their lives -- innocent lambs, all of them. They all pointed to him.

---

[15] Genesis 3:15
[16] John 1:29

So, when Yeshua heard or read the story of the first Passover when Moses was instructed by God to tell the people of Israel, enslaved in Egypt, to kill a *spotless lamb* and put *the blood of the lamb* on their doorposts as a *token* upon the houses in order to escape the death angel,[17] Yeshua knew that ultimately *that blood* was symbolic of his blood, and therefore symbolic of his death.[18] But even further back than that, when God made "*coats of skins*" as clothing for Adam and Eve's nakedness and shame after the fall in the Garden of Eden, those skins had to come from somewhere.[19]

"AND ALL THAT DWELL UPON THE EARTH SHALL WORSHIP HIM WHOSE NAMES ARE NOT WRITTEN IN THE BOOK OF LIFE OF THE LAMB SLAIN FROM THE FOUNDATION OF THE WORLD."

REVELATION 13:8

So Yeshua would become *the lamb slain from the foundation of the world,*[20] and he knew it. Yeshua knew very well what was to come as he prayed in Gethsemane: the accusations, the lies, the beating, the humiliation, and finally the cross – it had all been foretold *by the Spirit* of

---

[17] Exodus 12:1-13

[18] Hebrews 9:16-18. *Note*: Here, the author of Hebrews explicitly ties the **blood** of Yeshua to his **death** as a symbol of that death, connecting the legal force and/or application of a testament's testamentary terms to the *death of the testator*.

[19] Genesis 3:21

[20] Revelation 13:8, I Peter 1:20.

prophecy[21] in vivid detail one way or another. So as he prayed there in the garden, Yeshua knew he'd be tried by the Jewish leaders, given over to the Romans, treated like a criminal, spit upon, scourged, crucified, and unjustly put to death. It was fundamental, and had been from the beginning. Without the *shedding of innocent blood*[22] there could be no *remission of sins*.[23] Most of the Jewish religion was based on that symbol, the ending of a life, the shedding of blood, the death of an *innocent* as a *ransom payment*[24] for those who had sinned – it was crystal clear to our Savior, and always had been.

"BUT YOUR INIQUITIES HAVE SEPARATED BETWEEN YOU AND YOUR GOD..."

ISAIAH 59:2

But Yeshua had never sinned. He had never experienced a single moment of *separation* from his Father's presence. God's only begotten and *beloved* Son had always enjoyed unbroken, loving, wonderful communion and relationship with his God -- no gap, no emptiness, and no inner sense of aloneness. Yeshua was the *conduit* of the Spirit, the *True Vine*[25] in his Father's

---

[21] John 5:39, Revelation 19:10.See Also, Appendix: *The Prophets*

[22] Matthew 27:4

[23] Hebrews 9:22

[24] Hosea 13:11, Matthew 20:28, Mark 10:45, I Timothy 2:6.

Garden, a virtual *Tree of Life* coursing with the *eternal life*[26] of his Father inside. So the thought of being cut off from that *life,* the thought of taking on the sin of the world, the idea of becoming sin itself -- *cursed*[27] and dying as a criminal, abandoned by God's Spirit -- this was a foreboding unknown and an ominous idea and prospect. Yeshua had protected, cherished, and nurtured his *relationship* with his Father all his life -- and now it was to be taken away?

SEPARATION

In contrast, our own *innate* lack in this regard is self-evident, and we can trace the problem back to that other garden, *The Garden of Eden.* It wasn't until *after* Adam and Eve partook of the fruit of the *"Tree of the Knowledge of Good and Evil"* that they *realized* they were *naked* and felt *disconnected* from the God who created them.[28] This led to an immediate impulse to *cover up* (sew fig leaves together), *hide* from God (behind the trees of the garden), and react in *shame* (feel negatively about themselves).[29]

---

[25] John 15:1

[26] *Note*: In I John 3:15 our Apostle John speaks of eternal life dwelling within us, and in I John 5:11 John declares that this *eternal life* is in God's Son.

[27] Galatians 3:13

[28] Genesis 3:7

[29] Genesis 3:7-13

The word "death" comes from the root word for separation, and that's exactly what happened in Eden. Civilization itself has been impacted by the mere symbolism of this story, let alone the actual effect of the events themselves. Art, literature, human psychology, sociology, culture itself -- all affected by the hidden meaning encoded in this one series of events, written down and passed along from one generation to the next: disobedience, nakedness, shame, paradise lost, spiritual emptiness, and death. It is *who we are* after the Garden of Eden, after the so-called fall of man.

"FOR IN THIS WE GROAN, EARNESTLY DESIRING TO BE CLOTHED UPON WITH OUR HOUSE WHICH IS FROM HEAVEN."

II CORINTHIANS 5:2

After man's disobedience in the Garden of Eden there was a *gap* or *separation* between God and mankind, and between heaven and earth, and we all feel it and experience it in one form or another to this day. *As it is written*, God *drove* man out of the Garden and blocked man's access to the *Tree of Life* with a flaming sword.[30] From the very day that God drove Adam and Eve out of the *paradise of his presence* and away from the *Tree of Life*, literally *evicting* man from his *organic* abode,

---

[30] Genesis 3:24-25

separating him from the lush orchards and fruitful lands that God had allotted him -- mankind found himself empty and alone, *without form and void.*

It was a loss mankind would not recover from.[31] It sent shockwaves so deep into his *body, soul, and spirit* that every generation since has suffered with the internal, spiritual emptiness that came with it. The symptoms are persistent and pervasive on every level of life in our fallen world. They are part of our ancestral DNA, imprinted on our very identities, engraved on our subconscious, and carved deeply into our collective memory. *Spiritual homelessness* and longing are part of the *submerged iceberg* of who we are as a human race, and wherever we go, there we are.

One of the most thoughtful of our ancestors, King David, often described his own inner longing, saying: *"My soul longs, yes, even faints for the courts of the LORD; my heart and my flesh cry out for the living God...*[32] And again, *"You are my hiding place... "*[33] And yet again, *"For in the time of trouble he shall hide me in his pavilion; in*

---

[31] *Note:* All of mankind abides in death (separation from God) until Messiah's substitutionary death is accepted. Yeshua abolished death and separation from God for all those who *join themselves* to him.

[32] Psalm 84:1-3

[33] Psalm 32:7

the secret place of his tabernacle he shall hide me; he shall set me high upon a rock."[34]

We all seek a *hiding place*, a pavilion, a place in God's presence to fill *a void* within. Of course, some of us *know* this is what we are really looking for. But some of us don't. So we try to fill the void with anything and everything we think will help: alcohol, drugs, sex, money, career, relationships, praise from others, climbing mountains,[35] you name it we've tried it. We were driven out of *Eden* by God himself, barred from the *Tree of Life*, separated from our spiritual Father, spiritually disconnected from *Paradise*, and sentenced to live with a vacancy, an emptiness, a breach we inherited from *the man and woman* we all trace our ancestry back to.

Ever since the eviction from Garden of Eden we have felt like, and in fact have been, "*strangers and pilgrims*" on this earth, searching for a *spiritual homeland* we have lost. Spiritual need, spiritual longing, homelessness, a place to hide -- these are the *symptoms* of a universal condition we are all stricken by. As it is written of those who have gone before us, "*These all died in faith, not having received the promises, but having seen them afar*

---

[34] Psalm 27:5

[35] Of course, climbing mountains and the like is fine and wonderful if done to experience God's wonder and beauty as Creator.

*off were assured of them, embraced them and confessed that they were **strangers and pilgrims** on the earth. For those who say such things declare plainly that they seek a* **homeland.** "[36]

But Yeshua the Messiah was different. Yeshua was another kind of *Adam* altogether,[37] an Adam whose roots traced, not to the dust of the earth and a curse, but into heaven itself.[38] Yeshua had no emptiness, no void, no unmet longing, only the *paradise* of the eternal God living in *unbroken fellowship* within him. There was no submerged iceberg of loss, shame, and abandonment, only unconditional love and acceptance *permeated* his being.[39] Consider, then, the incalculable value of what our Master was being asked to willingly surrender in Gethsemane. It was a *relationship* that had sustained him each and every hour of his life, and now, upon request, his Father, his *Abba*,[40] his treasure, his *own pearl of great price*, was asking him to let it all go, to give it all up, to accept total

---

[36] Hebrews 11:13-14

[37] I Corinthians 15:45-49

[38] I Corinthians 15:47. *Note:* Yeshua's **human** paternal lineage traced to his Heavenly Father, and therefore to heaven, because his mother Mary conceived in her womb by the Holy Spirit, making God the Father of Yeshua. This sovereign act from heaven bridged the gap between God and man. Yeshua was also the Word made flesh, and that Word has its ultimate origin in heaven as well.

[39] John 15:10

[40] Mark 14:36, Romans 8:15, Galatians 4:6.

and unqualified separation, and to allow his human soul to fall cursed into the dark abyss of the dead. This required a depth of faith and trust that no man had ever approached.

THE FAITH OF THE SON OF GOD

The scriptures declare that *without faith it is impossible to please God.*[41] And of course, Yeshua of Nazareth had always **pleased** his Heavenly Father. Yeshua testified that *"he that sent me is with me: the Father has not left me alone; for I do always those things that **please** him."*[42] Similarly, the Father had spoken from heaven at Yeshua's baptism, declaring *"This is my beloved Son, in whom I am **well-pleased**."*[43] The scriptures also teach that *whatsoever is **not of faith** is sin.*[44] So the truth is, Yeshua lived by *faith*.

There was a reason for the blood and sweat in the *Garden of Gethsemane*. Yeshua of Nazareth had to emerge from his night in prayer with enough *faith and trust to weather the approaching storm.* He had to believe that throughout the remainder of the night and into morning -- through the trial, scourging, crucifixion, and whatever *time*

---

[41] Hebrews 11:6
[42] John 8:29
[43] Matthew 3:17
[44] Romans 14:23

he was alive hanging on the cross[45] -- he would remain trusting, pure in heart, sinless, and determined to finish his Father's work. Yeshua had to *believe* that even in this fiery furnace he would not falter – for what if he sinned in his heart at any point? What if he doubted? What would happen to his soul then? When his Father's Spirit left him, how would he react? Would this final test be too much to bear?

These were the subtle temptations, the questions, the nuances of his ordeal, the challenges of this trail of his obedience *and faith.* As it is written, *"I am crucified with Christ; nevertheless I live; yet not I, but Christ lives in me: and the life which I now live in the flesh I live by* **the faith of the Son of God,** *who loved me, and gave himself for me."*[46] And again, *"Looking unto Jesus, the* **author and finisher of faith;** *who for the joy that was set before him* **endured the cross,** *despising the shame, and is set down at the right hand of the throne of God."*[47] All of this took a personal courage, a *faith* and *trust* that none of us can truly imagine. Perhaps only Jonah knew even a shred of what was to come for our Savior.

---

[45] Indeed, Yeshua was challenged even on the cross by one of the criminals next to him. And of course, he responded in love.

[46] Galatians 2:20

[47] Hebrews 12:2

"FOR AS JONAH WAS THREE DAYS AND THREE NIGHTS IN THE WHALE'S BELLY; SO SHALL THE SON OF MAN BE THREE DAYS AND THREE NIGHTS IN THE HEART OF THE EARTH."

MATTHEW 12:40

And yet, all of this had been the Father's plan *from the beginning,* and there was no other option on the table, no other cup for Messiah to drink. Betrayal, trial, scourging, humiliation, crucifixion, abandonment, and death awaited Yeshua that night and morning. But it was the only way to fulfill the scriptures and the *eternal purpose* that our Heavenly Father had for mankind from the beginning.

As Yeshua himself explained to his disciples prior to his long night in Gethsemane, *"...the hour has come that the Son of man should be glorified. Truly, truly I say unto you, except a **corn of wheat** fall into the ground and die, it abides alone; but if it dies, it brings forth **much fruit**."*[48] Death and resurrection, *seed* and much fruit, the Son of man *glorified* -- this had been the *hidden wisdom*[49] ordained before the world to *our glory*, the *eternal purpose*[50] of God for mankind from the beginning -- and Yeshua knew his death was the key to all of it.

---

[48] John 12:23-24
[49] I Corinthians 2:7
[50] Ephesians 3:11

THE QUESTION

"I ADJURE YOU BY THE LIVING GOD THAT YOU TELL US WHETHER YOU ARE THE MESSIAH, THE SON OF GOD?"

MATTHEW 26:63

Of course, we know what happened that fateful night and following morning in Jerusalem after Gethsemane. There would be no rescue, no call for angels, and no deliverance from an undeserved death. Yeshua obeyed. Yeshua fulfilled. Yeshua carried his cross and finished his work. As it is written, *Judas*, one of his twelve disciples, would later show up in the garden with temple guards, chief priests, captains of the temple, and elders[51] -- kissing him on the cheek to betray his *identity* to his adversaries in the darkness of the hour.[52] They took Yeshua away, and he did not resist them. He was as a lamb led to the slaughter.[53]

The Gospels paint a dramatic picture. They organized a formal but illegal trial in the early morning hours. Yeshua was falsely accused, witnesses against him lied and could not agree with one another, and the process began to unravel. Finally, no doubt irritated with the proceedings, the High Priest himself asked Yeshua the

---

[51] Luke 22:52
[52] Luke 22:48
[53] Isaiah 53:7, Matthew 26:62-63.

relevant and final question, the one question that would seal his fate and lead to his death, and it could not have been a more fitting *bookend* to our Savior's life and ministry on earth.

During the temptation in the wilderness, Satan had framed the test of Yeshua with one repeated question; a question intended to illicit a personal defense of Messiah's position in creation: *"If you are the Son of God... If you are the Son of God"* (Luke 4:3, 9). Now, at the trial of Yeshua in Jerusalem, the High Priest would raise the same issue and use it to finally determine *Yeshua's* guilt and fate in the eyes of the orthodox. As it is written, *"I adjure you by the living God that you tell us whether you are the Christ, the Son of God?"*[54]

Our Savior's answer to that question[55] would reveal the fundamental issue and stone of stumbling for the religious orthodoxy to this very day – the startling nobility and exaltation of Yeshua's *humanity* in God's *eternal purpose*, and the place he has in his Father's heart, and at his Father's Right Hand, as *The Beloved*.

---

[54] Matthew 26:63

[55] *"You have said: nevertheless I say unto you, hereafter you shall see the Son of man sitting on the right hand of power, and coming in the clouds of heaven."* (Matthew 26:64).

CHAPTER FIVE

The Beloved

"BEHOLD MY SERVANT, WHOM I HAVE CHOSEN, MY BELOVED, IN WHOM
MY SOUL IS WELL PLEASED; I WILL PUT MY SPIRIT UPON HIM, AND HE
SHALL SHOW JUDGMENT TO THE NATIONS."

MATTHEW 12:18

WHEN YESHUA EMERGED from the waters of John's Baptism to officially begin his ministry, it is written that as he prayed *the heavens were opened* and the *Holy Spirit descended in a bodily form like a dove, abiding upon him* as a voice came from heaven declaring, *"You are my **beloved** Son; in you I am well pleased."*[1]

He was thirty years old. The Bible doesn't say much about his first thirty years of life, at least not directly. We know he was born in Bethlehem,[2] spent part of his early life in Egypt, and then moved to Nazareth.[3] We have a record of Yeshua at the age of twelve staying in Jerusalem while Mary and Joseph began to make their way back to Nazareth after observing the feast of Passover.[4] They were

---

[1] Luke 3:22
[2] Matthew 2:1
[3] Matthew 2:15, 20-23, Hosea 11:1.
[4] Luke 2:41-52

traveling in a large party and assumed Yeshua was with extended family, not realizing he had stayed behind in Jerusalem. Three days later they found him in the Temple.

Yeshua was found among the teachers and elders of Israel, amazing them with his insight and questions.[5] No one knows what the boy Yeshua did for those three days, where he slept, ate, etc., but based on the man he would one-day become it would not be a stretch to believe that he spent the entire time in the Temple – fasting, praying, hearing the elders, enjoying the time alone with his Father. Three days and three nights alone in Jerusalem would be a long time for any regular twelve-year-old; but Yeshua was different. His parents had no cause for concern, for as Yeshua told them -- they should have known he would be *in his Father's house*.[6]

TRADITIONS

While there is no historical written record[7] describing Yeshua's early life in any detail, it isn't difficult to put together a general profile of what that life would have been like for the *beloved Son* of God. For instance, we

---

[5] Luke 2:46-47

[6] Luke 2:49 NIV

[7] *Note*: It is this author's opinion that the Holy Bible is the only authoritative written record of the life of Messiah -- Apocryphal documents notwithstanding.

know that both he and his parents followed the Law of Moses, being obedient to the scriptures. As practicing Jews, their whole lives would have been guided by well-worn traditions and deeply held beliefs. As it is written: *"Hear O Israel: The LORD our God, the LORD is one. Love the LORD your God with all your heart and with all your soul and with all your strength. And these words that I command you today are to be upon your hearts. Impress them on your children..."*[8] This commandment would have carried great weight in the lives of Mary and Joseph, as well as in the life of their eldest son Yeshua.

The Law of Moses contemplates **itself** as the centerpiece of day-to-day life, the *commandments* of God being paramount: *"...talk about them when you sit at home and when you walk along the road, when you lie down and when you get up. Tie them as symbols on your hands and bind them on your foreheads. Write them on the doorframes of your houses and on your gates."* [9] So we don't have to wonder if Yeshua grew up familiar with the Law of Moses. Indeed, Yeshua would have grown up *delighting* in the Law. As it is written again, *"Blessed is the man who does not walk in the counsel of the wicked, or stand in the way of sinners, or sit in the seat of mockers.*

---

[8] Deuteronomy 6:4-7
[9] Deuteronomy 6:7-9

But his delight is in the law of the LORD, and on his law he meditates day and night. He is like a tree planted by streams of water, which yields its fruit in season and whose leaf does not wither. Whatever he does prospers."[10]

Yeshua lived by *every word* that came from his Father's mouth.[11] In fact, later during his ministry there were times when Yeshua's disciples pled with him to take a break and eat.[12] Yeshua responded that *he had meat to eat that they knew not of.*[13] The Law of Moses assumes obedience, not from obligation, but from pure and holy desire springing naturally from the heart. That desire would have characterized the life of Yeshua at every stage. Job once testified that he *esteemed the words of God's mouth more than his daily food.*[14] We can be certain that Yeshua felt that same hunger, and more. As it is written again, *"...behold, a virgin shall conceive and bear a son, and shall call his name Immanuel. Butter and honey shall he eat, that he may know to refuse the evil, and choose the good."*[15] Of course, the "butter and honey" of Yeshua's life was the Word of his Father, and of his God.[16]

---

[10] Psalm 1:1-3
[11] Luke 4:4
[12] John 4:31
[13] John 4:32
[14] Job 23:12
[15] Isaiah 7:14-15
[16] Revelation 3:12

So Yeshua grew up as an extraordinarily devoted Jew of first-century Palestine, of the tribe of Judah,[17] *"born of a woman, born under the law."*[18] He was raised in an orthodox Jewish home and was part of a traditional Jewish family where the God of Israel was *everything* and where the scriptures were read out loud daily, spoken of constantly, and committed to memory religiously – just as Moses commanded.

In Yeshua's home, tradition and heritage were valued, family was honored and respected, and the Word of God was treasured above all else. By blood Yeshua was related to John the Baptist, whose father was a priest and whose mother was a daughter of Aaron, both of whom were *righteous before God, walking in all the commandments of the Lord, blameless.*[19] Yeshua's mother Mary was of the house of David, *highly favored of God, and blessed among women.*[20] Yeshua's step-father Joseph was *a just man*, and also of the house of David.[21] In such a family a child was raised on the scriptures, attended Synagogue, celebrated feasts, Sabbaths, and holy days. This was the landscape of

---

[17] Hebrews 7:14, Revelation 5:5.
[18] Galatians 4:4
[19] Luke 1:5-6
[20] Luke 1:28-32
[21] Matthew 1:19-20

Yeshua's day-to-day life growing up in Israel, surrounded by a devout culture and family.

YESHUA'S BRETHREN

It is written that in his early years, Yeshua *"grew in wisdom and stature and in favor with God and man."*[22] Luke records that Yeshua *"waxed strong in spirit, filled with wisdom; and the grace of God was upon him."*[23] He was Mary's firstborn son, but she went on to have other sons[24] and daughters.[25] We don't know much about Yeshua's siblings, though we can read a little about his brothers in the Gospels here and there. It is clear they were initially reluctant to accept him as the Messiah.[26] In fact, it wasn't until his resurrection from the dead that his brothers accepted him.[27] This is a telling fact. Yeshua would testify that *a prophet is not without honor, save in his own country, and in his own house.*[28] So as a boy, in his teen years, and no doubt throughout his twenties, Yeshua's *favor with God and man* would have stood out.

---

[22] Luke 2:52

[23] Luke 2:40

[24] Matthew 13:55, 12:46-47, 28:10, Mark 3:31, John 2:12, 7:3-5, Acts 1:14

[25] Mark 6:3 (*sisters*)

[26] John 7:5

[27] Galatians 1:19 (*Note*: James, Yeshua's brother, authored the Epistle of James).

[28] Matthew 13:57

Once Yeshua began his prophetic and Messianic ministry, however, things changed dramatically. As it is written, *"He came unto his own, but his own did not receive him.*[29] And as Isaiah had prophesied hundreds of years earlier: *"...he shall grow up before him as a tender plant, And as a root out of dry ground. He has no form or comeliness; and when we see him, there is no beauty that we should desire him. He is **despised and rejected by men**, a man of sorrows and acquainted with grief. And we hid, as it were, our faces from him; he was despised, and we **did not esteem him.**"*[30]

The rejection of Yeshua[31] of Nazareth was also foreshadowed in the story of Joseph in the Book of Genesis. It wasn't until Joseph revealed his *prophetic dreams* to his **brethren** that his brethren began to despise him. As it is written, *"Please hear this dream which I have dreamed: We were binding sheaves in the field. Then behold, my sheaf arose and also stood upright; and indeed your sheaves stood all around and bowed down to my sheaf."*

"And his brothers said to him, Shall you indeed reign over us? Or shall you indeed have dominion over us?" So

---

[29] John 1:11

[30] Isaiah 53:2-3

[31] Matthew 8:34, 21:42, Mark 6:3, Luke 4:28-29, 17:25, 23:18, John 12:48.

they hated him even more for his dreams and for his words. "[32]

We might imagine how Yeshua's own brethren felt when news of his anointing and calling began to spread -- a voice from heaven, a dove descending from above, a beloved Son in whom God was well-pleased – really? Sibling rivalry because of a *favored status in God's eyes* went as far back as the first two brothers, Cain and Abel.[33]

In Joseph's case, his brothers would ultimately conspire to kill him[34] by throwing him into a pit. But Joseph was later sold to Ishmaelite's for 20 pieces of silver, brought to Egypt as a slave, imprisoned, miraculously set free, and raised to great prominence and favor in the house of Pharaoh.[35] Years later, when a famine struck the entire region, Joseph's brethren were forced into Egypt to seek food. As it is written, *"Now Joseph was governor over the land...and Joseph's brothers came and bowed down before him with their faces to the earth, and Joseph recognized his brothers, but they did not recognize him."*[36] So there they were, bowing

---

[32] Genesis 37:6-11

[33] Genesis 4:1-16; Hebrews 11:4. *Note*: According to the Apostle John, Cain was *"of that wicked one"* (I John 3:12). Yeshua calls Satan *"a murderer from the beginning"* (John 8:44). Consequently, we know *exactly* who was behind the murder of Abel.

[34] Genesis 37:18-28

[35] Genesis 38-42

down to their own brother who had risen to Pharaoh's *right hand* in the kingdom, still not recognizing him as their brother, but totally dependent upon him none-the-less.

And so it is written of Yeshua of Nazareth, the favored and exalted brother of us all -- *"For both he that sanctifies and they who are sanctified **are all of one**: for which cause he is not ashamed to call them **brethren.** "*[37] Yeshua calls those of us who believe in him, *brethren.* Yeshua has been **exalted** *to our Father's right hand as an overcomer -- to be a Prince, Savior, and Judge.*[38] Yeshua has been **given** *all power in heaven and earth.*[39] The scriptures are clear that Yeshua has been given *a name above every name*[40] by our Heavenly Father, which speaks of his **relative** positioning among man[41] and angel.[42] And, just like Joseph, our Heavenly Father now requires that *all men come to Yeshua* for their needs.[43] None of us can come to our Father, or even honor our Father,[44] except

---

[36] Genesis 42:6, 8

[37] Hebrews 2:11

[38] Acts 5:31, Acts 10:42, 17:31.

[39] Matthew 28:18

[40] Philippians 2:9-11

[41] Philippians 2:9

[42] Hebrews 1:4-5

[43] John 15:5, John 14:6.

[44] John 5:23

through Yeshua[45] – our exalted, honored, and noble *brother.*

It took some time, but Joseph did finally *reveal himself* to his own brethren; and when they finally recognized him *as their brother*[46] they wept for joy, no doubt repenting profusely. The same will be true of Yeshua's revealing to his church.[47] As it is written: *"Until we all come unto the unity of the faith and of the knowledge of the Son of God, unto a **perfect man**, unto the measure of the stature of the fullness of Christ."*[48]

YESHUA'S CHARACTER

Of course, there would have been a noticeable maturity about Yeshua as he came of age in Nazareth, as well as an extraordinary depth of character. As we've already seen, Isaiah wrote of that depth in another Messianic prophecy, saying: *"There shall come forth a Rod from the stem of Jesse, and a Branch shall grow out of his roots. The Spirit of the LORD shall rest upon Him, the Spirit of wisdom and understanding, the Spirit of counsel and might, the Spirit of knowledge and of the fear*

---

[45] John 14:6

[46] Genesis 45:1-15

[47] Ephesians 1:16-23, 3:14-21. (*Note*: Paul's underlying assumption in his writings is that all believers need a growing awareness and understanding of Christ).

[48] Ephesians 4:13

of the LORD. His delight is in the fear of the LORD, and He shall not judge by the sight of His eyes, nor decide by the hearing of His ears; but with righteousness He shall judge the poor, and decide with equity for the meek of the earth..."[49]

Isaiah's words provide great insight into the character of our Savior. The Spirit of the LORD would *rest* upon him, and he would *delight* in the fear of the LORD. This is a powerful combination of traits in any man. Further, Yeshua would be *anointed* with wisdom, understanding, and knowledge **by the Spirit** -- this would not come from himself. Yeshua would not judge by his natural senses, not by his intellect, common sense, or even his conscience -- but only *by the Spirit* that indwelled him.

So Yeshua once testified, *"The words that I speak to you I do not speak on my own authority; but the Father who dwells in me does the works."*[50] And again, *"I can of my own self do nothing."*[51] John the Baptist would say of Yeshua: *"For he whom God has sent speaks the words of God, for God gives not the Spirit by measure unto him."*[52] Indeed, as stated earlier it was the *anointing of* the Spirit

---

[49] Isaiah 11:1-4
[50] John 14:10
[51] John 5:19, 30
[52] John 3:34

of God that made Yeshua who and what he was. As it is written, *"The Spirit of the Lord is upon me, because he has* **anointed** *me to preach the gospel to the poor; he has sent me to heal the brokenhearted, to preach deliverance to the captives, and recovering of sight to the blind, to set at liberty them that are bruised, to preach the acceptable year of the Lord."*[53]

That anointing, however, does not accompany every type of person. The scriptures declare that God *dwells* in the high and holy place -- but also with him who is of a *contrite spirit.*[54] This speaks explicitly of someone's humility and character as the *conduit* for God's presence. So in his day, Moses was described as the *meekest man on earth.*[55] It is no wonder, then, that Moses was sometimes so close to God that his face literally glowed with God's presence and glory.[56] Yeshua, too, was of the *meekest* character and disposition. *"Take my yoke upon you and learn of me,"* Yeshua would testify, *"for I am meek and lowly in heart, and you shall find rest for your souls."*[57] In our Messiah Yeshua we find a perfect *example* of a

---

[53] Luke 4:18-19, Isaiah 61:1

[54] Isaiah 57:15

[55] Numbers 12:3

[56] Exodus 34:33-35, II Corinthians 3:13-15.

[57] Matthew 11:29

yielded conduit -- a *True Vine*[58] for *the Spirit* and *life* of God to flow through.

This is important. As stated above, the Spirit of the LORD *rested* upon Yeshua. Yeshua was fully *yielded* to his Father's Spirit, and in Yeshua God found no *resistance* to his Spirit. So the scriptures declare that man fulfills *the Sabbath* only when we *cease from our own labors.*[59] This is the *fulfillment* of *the rest* God has commanded, of the Sabbath we are to observe. Yeshua *obeyed* that commandment just as certainly as he obeyed all of God's commandments.[60] Yeshua walked and lived in the *rest* of God -- a place of *perfect spiritual rest* as the Spirit of the LORD flowed through him effortlessly.[61] Indeed, Yeshua's entire mission was to humble himself and *empty himself*[62] so that his Heavenly Father could *fully indwell him.*[63] So when our Master Yeshua tells us to *find rest* for our souls *in him,* in his *meekness* and *humility,* he is showing us the pathway to fulfilling the very commandments of God.[64] He is also providing a schematic

---

[58] John 15:1

[59] Hebrews 4:1-11

[60] Genesis 2:3, Exodus 16:23, Exodus 20:1-17.

[61] Yeshua would testify that the Sabbath was made for man, not man for the Sabbath (Matthew 12:8). He also testified that the Son of Man was Lord of the Sabbath (Mark 2:27).

[62] Philippians 2:4-9

[63] John 3:34

for tapping into the *life of God* as we *abide* in him, and his words abide in us.[65] As it is written, "*I am the vine, you are the branches; he that abides in me, and I in him, the same brings forth much fruit: for without me you can do nothing.*"[66]

HERE IS WISDOM

The epistle of James tells us that "...*the wisdom that is from above is first pure, then peaceable, gentle, willing to yield, full of mercy and good fruits, without partiality and without hypocrisy.*"[67] It is no wonder that this description of *wisdom* happens also to be a perfect description of Yeshua himself -- pure, peaceable, gentle, willing to yield, full of mercy and good fruits, without partiality or hypocrisy. Indeed, the Apostle Paul would describe Yeshua as "*the wisdom of God.*"[68]

The scriptures also testify that *God is love.*[69] And in his first epistle to the Corinthians, Paul describes the very *character of love* -- longsuffering, not puffed up, without envy, not self-seeking, not easily provoked, without evil

---

[64] Romans 6:4, 8:1, II Corinthians 6:16, Galatians 5:16, Colossians 2:6.
[65] John 6:63, John 6:68, John 15:7.
[66] John 15:5
[67] James 3:17
[68] I Corinthians 1:24
[69] I John 4:8

thoughts, rejoicing in truth, bearing all, believing all, hoping and enduring through all[70] -- this also is the *character* of Yeshua. It is the *fruit* of an *emptied life surrendered to our Heavenly Father*, a life of self-denial, humility, complete devotion, and immersion in the *Spirit* and *Word* of Almighty God.

So this was the *Messiah*, the *perfect man* who emerged from the waters of John's Baptism to the *delight* of his Father – a meek, humble, pure, gentle, guile-less man – the perfect conduit for God to flow through. So of course, he was *God's Beloved*.

THE BELOVED

Whenever and whatever the God of Israel spoke, whether those words were written on parchment or whispered in the ear by the Spirit, we can be sure that Yeshua of Nazareth hung on each and every word. Yeshua's *"eye was single,"* so his whole body was *full of light*.[71] Yeshua walked in complete trust and faith, and marveled when others could not believe.[72] When Yeshua read the twenty-third Psalm he trusted that his *Father* was *his Shepherd,* that he would always be safe and provided

---

[70] I Corinthians 13:4-7
[71] Matthew 6:22
[72] Mark 6:4-6

for, and that goodness and mercy would follow him all the days of his life. Yeshua grounded his entire life on the Word of God -- every promise, every warning, and every admonition. As it is written: *"Because you have made the LORD, which is my refuge, even the Most High, your habitation, there shall no evil befall you...for he shall give his angels charge over you, to keep you in all your ways."*[73] This was and is[74] our *beloved* Messiah, and God's *beloved* Son.

If ever a man loved God with all his heart, soul, and strength; if ever a man delighted in, meditated upon, and spoke about the law of his God; if ever a man rested in the shadow of the Almighty or made the LORD his refuge, shelter, and fortress, it was Yeshua of Nazareth, God's *beloved*. No one in the history of the world enjoyed a star-lit night, a sunset, a lily of the field, or the innocence of a child more than Yeshua. If anyone honored his father and mother, it was Yeshua. If anyone kept his heart from covetousness, it was Yeshua. If anyone meditated on God's law day and night, it was Yeshua.

How rare was it that this man loved his heavenly Father from a pure heart? How rare was it that this man said *not my will*, but *your will* be done -- even as he was

---

[73] Psalm 91:9-11
[74] Hebrews 13:8

being asked to endure a death none of us can understand? It is written that *"all have sinned and come short of the glory of God."*[75] And yet, throughout his life and ministry, through the *Garden of Gethsemane*, to the cross, and even to the abyss of death, Yeshua never sinned -- no not once. Yeshua walked in *perfect harmony* with his God and Father through trials and testing that truly defy the imagination. Yeshua loved his God with all his strength, loved his neighbor as himself,[76] and followed with his **whole heart** both the letter and the spirit of the entire Law of Moses to the bitter end – to the pouring out of his soul. *"Hear, O Israel; the LORD our God is one LORD: and you shall love the Lord your God with all your heart, and with all your soul, and with all your might."*[77] This, the first and great commandment -- was *obeyed* from *the heart* and *soul* by Yeshua of Nazareth, the *spotless* Lamb of God.

Imagine, then, that *beloved* soul! Imagine how the Father would want to reward such a person, and how any Father, but especially *this* Father, would cherish and even treasure the devotion and love of such a person! God is the *Habitation of Justice*, so how might that just God respond

---

[75] Romans 3:23; *See also*, Romans 3:10-18.

[76] Luke 10:27, Romans 13:9-10, James 2:8.

[77] Deuteronomy 6:4-5

to the holiness of the *only man* to ever love him and obey him? This is our Father's *beloved*, and this is our exalted and honored brother.

God had created and loved mankind only to watch all of mankind turn away from him – every single human being ever born would turn away from God and follow his or her own pathway, their own will, and their own selfish desires. But this *man Yeshua, this last Adam,* this *beloved Son* was different. In Yeshua God saw the tender *first-fruits* of his garden -- true righteousness, heart-holiness, and reciprocated love and devotion – from a human soul and character no less! The truth is – Yeshua's human soul is *priceless* to God's heart.

Our beloved Savior was not a precious stone taken from a heavenly palace and placed in the human realm for all to wonder at and admire. Make no mistake, Yeshua's rare and noble character, his priceless soul, his very identity and being were *forged* in the fires of trial, temptation, challenge, and even torture and death. Yeshua of Nazareth was *made perfect through sufferings.*[78] He is a precious stone formed in the pressures and heat of *a battle of life* that none of us can imagine. We get a rare glimpse of this perfected soul in Gethsemane, blood dripping from

---

[78] Hebrews 2:10

his pores as he prays in anguish, fighting until everything he was and everything he had was surrendered to his God. And then we see him suffer -- tried as a criminal, scourged, beaten, humiliated, and then nailed to a wooden cross only to have the Spirit of God depart from him as he who knew no sin *took on the sins of the world.* Worthy, worthy, worthy is *the Lamb* that was slain!

"AND THEY SANG A NEW SONG, SAYING, YOU ARE WORTHY TO TAKE THE BOOK, AND TO OPEN THE SEALS THEREOF: FOR YOU WERE SLAIN, AND HAVE REDEEMED US TO GOD BY YOUR BLOOD OUT OF EVERY KINDRED, AND TONGUE, AND PEOPLE, AND NATION."

REVELATION 5:9

David once asked, *"Who may ascend into the hill of the LORD? Or who may stand in His holy place?"* The answer was simple: *"He who has **clean hands** and a **pure heart.**"*[79] None of us can say that we meet this standard, no not one. None of us has clean hands. None of us has a pure heart. None of us may *stand in the holy place* in ourselves. None of us may ascend into the hill of the LORD.

But the man Yeshua did ascend that hill, and now he stands in *the Holy Place* as Lord, the Son of Man at the Right Hand of God, *King and Priest.*

---

[79] Psalm 24:3-4

CHAPTER SIX

King and Priest

PILATE THEREFORE SAID UNTO HIM, *"ARE YOU A KING THEN?"* YESHUA
ANSWERED, *"YOU SAY RIGHTLY THAT I AM A KING. FOR THIS CAUSE I WAS
BORN AND FOR THIS CAUSE I HAVE COME INTO THE WORLD, THAT I
SHOULD BEAR WITNESS TO THE TRUTH.* EVERYONE THAT IS OF THE
TRUTH HEARS MY VOICE"

JOHN 18:37

WHEN YESHUA'S DISCIPLES asked him to teach them to pray, Yeshua's *prayer* reflected his own vision, mission, and purpose in life. He began, *"Our Father **in heaven**, hallowed be your name, **your kingdom come**, your will be done **on earth** as it is in heaven...."*[1] These were the threads that formed the fabric of Yeshua's life and identity -- his Father's *name*, his Father's *kingdom*, and his Father's *will* done on earth. They reflect the heart of a Prince, the man who was born to be King. Yeshua would close his prayer to the Father in the same vein, saying, *"For thine is the power, and the kingdom, and the glory forever, amen."*[2] Yeshua of Nazareth, *the Son of David*, was foreordained to ascend to a throne; but neither man

---

[1] Matthew 6:9-10
[2] Matthew 6:13

nor angel knew just how vast and powerful that throne was destined to become.

THE THRONE OF DAVID

"...AND I WILL ESTABLISH HIS THRONE FOREVER. I WILL BE HIS FATHER, AND HE SHALL BE MY SON...AND I WILL ESTABLISH HIM IN MY HOUSE AND IN MY KINGDOM FOREVER; AND HIS THRONE SHALL BE ESTABLISHED FOREVER."

I CHRONICLES 17:12-14

By the time of Yeshua's birth in Bethlehem, the return of the kingdom to Israel had almost become a myth in the eyes of many who hoped in a Messiah. They waited for a conquering King -- the *Seed of David* who was to rule on David's Throne and restore the prominence and prestige of Israel over the nations. The glory of Israel had long since disappeared and Israel had become one of many vassal states of the Roman Empire. Rome had occupied Israel for generations, and while the Caesars had allowed Israel to maintain its own line of puppet rulers, as well as its religious traditions, the Roman soldiers in the streets, not to mention the tax collectors, were a constant reminder of Roman domination. But even under such conditions many still hoped in *the promise* that God made to David,[3] that *of his lineage* God would raise up *a king* who they believed would rise up against Rome and restore the

---

[3] II Samuel 22:51, I Chronicles 17:11-15.

kingdom to Israel.[4] But our Heavenly Father had something much bigger *in mind* when he ordained and minted the throne that *"The Son of David"* would one day rule from. The pathway to that throne, however, would be long and quite dramatic.

From the beginning, our Heavenly Father knew that Adam and Eve would fall, that Satan would become man's adversary, that man's heart would become corrupt, and that *all of the kingdoms of this world*[5] would eventually fall into Satan's hands after mankind surrendered his birthright. This meant that if a righteous kingdom was ever going to be established on earth *through man,*[6] it would have to be established with a repurchase and *repossession* of man's dominion. *"Thy kingdom come, thy will be done on earth as it is in heaven,"* therefore, was a tall order. This challenge was complicated by man's continued *free will* to enlist in whatever causes he chose, but also by the innate limitations[7] in man after the fall.

---

[4] Acts 1:6

[5] Luke 4:5-6. II Corinthians 4:4.

[6] Mankind was created to have a special kind of dominion, a dominion that was expressly *his own,* but one that also flowed from God's own dominion and sovereignty as man's Heavenly Father. Restoring that dominion, therefore, required the establishment of a human throne that would act as an *extension* of God's throne.

[7] II Corinthians 4:4. *Note:* Spiritual blindness was the direct result of man's partaking of the *Tree of the Knowledge of Good and Evil.* From the fall forward, Satan was able to "blind the mind" of mankind, and in that blindness take him

But the extension of our Father's *heavenly authority* and *sovereign will into the earth* through mankind was also complicated by the nature, structure, and complexity of Satan's spiritual kingdom and jurisdiction. *From the beginning* our Heavenly Father had created vast numbers of angels with various ranks, gifting, and spiritual influence and power.[8] When Satan rebelled against God's plan for man he took untold numbers of those angels with him, Satan being their prince. These angels retained their *spiritual rank* and power in the heavenly realm vis-à-vis man's fallen condition. Consequently, the complete *repossession* of man's birthright and dominion required the ascent of man, not only to an earthly throne to rule over earthly matters,[9] but to a sufficiently *high seat* in the *heavenly realm*, a position higher than all the angels, fallen and unfallen.[10]

From the foundation of the world, therefore, our Heavenly Father *ordained and minted* an Eternal Kingdom for his *Sons and Daughters[11]* -- a kingdom that would have its highest seat in heaven but would also have a presence on earth, a *beachhead* that would act as a staging area for

---

captive (II Timothy 2:26).

[8] Ephesians 6:12

[9] Isaiah 9:6-7

[10] Hebrews 1:4-5

[11] Matthew 25:34

the eventual occupation and overthrow of Satan's kingdom on earth, and in the spirit realm. This extension of the *Kingdom of Heaven* would *originate*[12] with a promise to Eve[13] and later to Abraham,[14] Isaac,[15] and Jacob,[16] *take root* on earth through the twelve tribes of Israel, find a mere *shadow* of its ultimate destiny through David and later Solomon, and finally come to *full-flower* in and through the Messiah, *a man* whose *maternal* lineage[17] traced to David but whose *paternal lineage and birthright* traced to God himself.[18]

This *dual-lineage* of the man Yeshua would provide him with a seat of authority and power of the highest rank in heaven by *inheritance* -- and on earth by *promise*. Thus, *all power in heaven **and** earth*[19] would ultimately come into the hands of a *second Adam*, bringing *mankind* once again into *Sonship dominion*. The throne and the kingdom of David would thereafter expand and extend into all the earth,[20] but its highest seat would be in heaven at *the Right*

---

[12] *Note:* Man's spiritual dominion actually originated when God made man in his own image and gave him dominion.

[13] Genesis 3:15

[14] Genesis 17:1-7

[15] Romans 9:7-10

[16] Genesis 28:12-15, 32:24-30.

[17] Matthew 1:1-16, Luke 3:23-38.

[18] Luke 1:31, 35.

[19] Matthew 28:18

[20] Isaiah 9:7, Daniel 2:44, Daniel 7:14, II Peter 1:11, Revelation 11:15.

Hand of God[21]*as angels and authorities and powers were made subject* to its occupant.[22]

All of this was planned, promised, and **ordained** from the beginning for mankind – by the *Habitation of Justice*, the God who sees the end from the beginning.

THE PROPHETS

"SEARCH THE SCRIPTURES; FOR IN THEM YOU THINK YOU HAVE ETERNAL LIFE: AND THEY TESTIFY OF ME."

JOHN 5:39

The Kingdom of God *extended to the earth* through mankind would take generations, even thousands of years. It would be built upon promises believed, traditions adhered to, territory re-taken, enemies defeated, worldliness resisted, angels fighting on man's behalf, and overcoming faith in the blood of the Lamb. Men and women would live their entire lives hoping in the promise, and believing in their hope, only to die with its fulfillment generations into the future.[23] Still, none of them would hope in vain.[24] All of the sufferings of the present life

---

[21] Note: The foreordained position at the Father's right hand was always intended for a human occupant, an only *begotten* Son and legal heir.

[22] I Peter 3:22, Colossians 2:15.

[23] Hebrews 11:13

[24] I Corinthians 2:9, Hebrews 11:16.

would be more than off-set by what our Heavenly Father had prepared for us.[25] In the meantime, however, our Father would keep the promise *alive* in the hearts of his people through the prophets.

Using symbol and metaphor, God would describe the kingdom that was to come in a variety of ways, subtly *foreshadowing* all of its dimensions with the skill of a painter. The prophet Daniel would speak of "*a stone cut out of a mountain*" without hands, a stone that would destroy the kingdoms of this world only to become a mountain itself.[26] As it is written, "*Then was the iron, the clay, the brass, the silver, and the gold broken to pieces together, and became like the chaff of the summer threshing floors; and the wind carried them away that no place was found for them; and the stone that smote the image became a great mountain and filled the whole earth.*"[27]

The prophet Zechariah would speak of a branch of a tree, a priest, a temple, and a throne, saying: "*Thus says the LORD of hosts...Behold, **the man** whose name is the BRANCH! From his place he shall branch out, and he shall build the temple of the LORD; yes, he shall build the*

---

[25] Id.

[26] Daniel 2:35-45

[27] Daniel 2:35

*temple of the LORD. He shall bear the glory, **and shall sit and rule on his throne**; so he shall be a **priest** on his throne, and the counsel of peace shall be between them both.*"[28]

The prophet Ezekiel would speak similarly of a *tender twig* becoming a great cedar tree. As it is written, *"Thus says the Lord GOD: I will take also one of the highest branches of the high cedar and set it out. I will crop off from the topmost of its young twigs **a tender one**, and will plant it on a high and prominent mountain. On the mountain height **of Israel** I will plant it; and it will bring forth boughs, and **bear fruit**, and be **a majestic cedar.** Under it will dwell birds of every sort; in the shadow of its branches they will dwell. And all the trees of the field shall know that I, the LORD, have brought down the high tree and **exalted the low tree**, dried up the green tree and made the dry tree flourish; I, the LORD, have spoken **and have done it.**"*[29]

The Messiah, himself a prophet,[30] would draw very directly on Ezekiel's prophecy of the *majestic cedar* in his own discussions of the Kingdom of God, comparing the kingdom to *the seed* of a mustard tree. As it is written,

---

[28] Zechariah 6:12-13

[29] Ezekiel 17:22-24

[30] Deuteronomy 18:15, 18; Matthew 13:57, 21:11; Luke 24:19, Acts 3:22, 7:37.

"The kingdom of heaven is like a grain of mustard seed, which a man took, and sowed in his field; which is indeed the least of all seeds, but when it is grown, it is the greatest among herbs, and becomes a tree, so that the birds of the air come and lodge in the branches thereof."[31] Yeshua would also refer to himself as a stone,[32] a vine,[33] and of course -- the Temple of God.[34]

But whether the symbol was a *stone* that became a *great mountain*, a *tender twig* that became a *great tree*, or a *man* who builds the Temple of the LORD and rules upon his throne *as a priest* -- these are just a few of the examples of the prophecies of the Kingdom of Heaven and of *the man* who would become king and rule upon the Throne of David.

OUR HIGH PRIEST

The author of the book of Hebrews would sum up his discussion of the Messiah this way: *"Now of the things which we have spoken, this is the sum: We have such a **high priest** who is set on **the right hand** of the throne of the Majesty in the heavens, a minister of the sanctuary,*

---

[31] Matthew 13:31-32, Mark 4:31, Luke 13:19.
[32] Matthew 21:42, Luke 20:17-18.
[33] John 15:1
[34] John 2:19-21

and of the true tabernacle, which the Lord pitched and not man."[35] He would go on to testify: *"But **this man**, after he had offered one sacrifice for sins forever, **sat down** on the **right hand** of God; from henceforth **expecting** till his **enemies** be made his footstool."*[36]

"YOU HAVE ASCENDED ON HIGH, YOU HAVE LED CAPTIVITY CAPTIVE: YOU HAVE RECEIVED GIFTS FOR MEN; YES, FOR THE REBELLIOUS ALSO, THAT THE LORD MIGHT DWELL AMONG THEM."

PSALM 68:18

Of course, the author of Hebrews would also add that this man, this same *high priest*, learned *obedience* through suffering,[37] was *made perfect* through suffering,[38] and was *tempted* on all points yet without sin.[39] And, because he was tempted, our high priest now has the ability to be *touched by the feeling of our infirmities* – making him a *more able* high priest.[40] This was the foreordained destiny of the last Adam Yeshua *from the beginning*, to be an empathetic, compassionate *high priest* and *king*.

So Peter would stand up on the Day of Pentecost and testify to the Jews: *"Men of Israel, hear these words: Jesus*

---

[35] Hebrews 8:1-2
[36] Hebrews 10:12-13
[37] Hebrews 5:8
[38] Hebrews 2:10
[39] Hebrews 4:15
[40] Hebrews 2:17-18

*of Nazareth, **a man attested** by God to you by miracles, wonders, and signs which God did **through Him** in your midst, as you yourselves also know -- him, being delivered by the determined **purpose** and **foreknowledge** of God, you have taken by lawless hands, have crucified, and put to death...."*

*"This Jesus God has raised up, of which we are all witnesses. Therefore **being exalted** to the **right hand of God,** and having **received** from the Father **the promise** of the Holy Spirit, **he poured out this** which you now see and hear. For David did not ascend into the heavens, but he says himself: The L*ord* said to my Lord, sit at my right hand, till I make **your enemies your footstool**. Therefore let all the house of Israel know assuredly that **God has made** this same Jesus, whom you crucified, **both Lord and Christ.**"*[41]

And later to the Gentiles Peter would proclaim: *"God **anointed** Jesus of Nazareth with the Holy Spirit and with power: **who went about doing good**, and healing all that were oppressed of the devil; for **God was with him.**"*[42] In both of these examples Peter's thinking is evident in his words: Yeshua was and is *"a man approved of God"* who

---

went about doing good and delivering people from Satan's grip – for "*God was with him.*"

Isaiah once prophesied, "*I will fasten him as a peg in a secure place, and he will become* **a glorious throne to his father's house.** *They will hang upon him* **all the glory** *of his father's house, the offspring and the posterity, all the vessels of small quantity, from the cups to all the pitchers.*"[43] This precisely states the role of Yeshua in his Father's Kingdom – a **Son** upon whom a Father puts his **own** honor and glory. Yeshua himself declared, "*That all men should honor the Son, even as they honor the Father. He that honors not the Son honors not the Father who has sent him.*"[44]

"*Are you a king then?*" Pilate would ask Yeshua before sending him to his death. Yeshua responded: "*You say rightly that I am a king. For this cause* **I was born** *and for this cause I have come into the world, that I should bear witness to the truth.*"[45] The angel *Gabriel* had announced this same glorious message to Yeshua's mother Mary before Yeshua was *conceived* in her womb: "*He shall be great, and shall be called the Son of the Highest, and the Lord God shall give unto him* **the throne of his**

---

[43] Isaiah 22:23-24
[44] John 5:23
[45] John 18:37

father David. And he shall reign over the house of Jacob forever, and of his kingdom there shall be no end. "[46]

So, after his resurrection and before he ascended to the **right hand** of his Father, Yeshua would testify: *"All power is **given** unto me in heaven and in earth. Go therefore, and teach all nations, baptizing them in the name of the Father, and of the Son, and of the Holy Spirit. Teaching them to observe all things whatsoever I have commanded you: and behold, I am with you always, even unto the end of the world."*[47]

This had been our Heavenly Father's *eternal purpose* from the beginning: **his kingdom come**, his **will** done on earth as it is **in heaven** – through mankind, through his Sons and Daughters -- still and always the heart of a Prince born to be King.

Of course, Yeshua also taught us that the Kingdom of God does not come *with observation*. He compared it to a *seed*, planted and left to grow on its own into whatever it was destined to become.[48] Yeshua also taught that the Kingdom of God was within us,[49] and that his Kingdom was not of this world.[50] Because ultimately, our Heavenly

---

[46] Luke 1:32-33

[47] Matthew 28:18-20

[48] Mark 4:26; Luke 13:18-19. See Also, I Corinthians 15:36-38.

[49] Luke 17:21

[50] John 18:36

Father's Kingdom is only established *on earth* as each of us allows *his will* to be done through us individually and collectively *as **the body*** and ***kingdom*** of Messiah. We do that by *abiding in Yeshua* as branches of the True Vine -- and we abide in that True Vine by coming to know him through reading, hearing, and applying his teachings in our daily lives as disciples, allowing him to *dwell in our hearts* through faith *by the Spirit*. When we do that, the Son of God, the Promised Seed of Creation, will take care of the rest as he dwells in us.

"FOR SUCH A HIGH PRIEST BECAME US, WHO IS HOLY, HARMLESS, UNDEFILED, SEPARATE FROM SINNERS, AND MADE HIGHER THAN THE HEAVENS."

HEBREWS 7:2

CHAPTER SEVEN

The Son of God

"AND THE HIGH PRIEST ANSWERED AND SAID UNTO HIM, I ADJURE YOU
BY THE LIVING GOD THAT YOU TELL US WHETHER YOU ARE THE
CHRIST, THE SON OF GOD?"

MATTHEW 26:63

FROM THE BEGINNING, our Heavenly Father's *eternal purpose* was that his honor, nobility, and dominion be reflected in mankind, bringing meaning to *the position* of *Sons and Daughters* in creation. So when Adam and Eve fell in *the Garden of Eden*, when shame and nakedness caused them to hide from the very God who created them, that relationship, that bond, that Father-Child reflection that was man's *purpose*, had to be restored legally, spiritually, and physically -- because without it man would forever dwell in darkness as fallen angels ruled the world.

But the restoration of God's *relationship* with mankind was *always* going come through a *second Adam*, a *promised seed*, a descendant *of Eve* whose own *bond*, whose own *relationship* with the Heavenly Father was whole and unbroken. The scales of justice had tipped with the sin and death of the first Adam, so it would take the righteousness and bodily resurrection of a second Adam to re-balance them again.[1] This would begin with a very special moment in the history of mankind, a moment that would produce an only *begotten human* Son of God, a man with a *birthright* so profound that it would try the hearts of his brethren. A virgin would conceive.[2] The child's father would be God himself. Angels would bow before him.[3] The wind and the sea would obey him.[4] The Father would completely fill him.[5] His name would carry the honor and nobility of the one who gave it to him.[6] He would empty himself[7] and be made perfect through suffering.[8] Then he would present himself as a *spotless lamb* to those who would sentence him to death for *who* and *what* he was.[9]

If such a child was *conceived* with such a *birthright*, with a literal *human lineage* that traced to God himself, and if his nobility remained untarnished by sin as he followed through with *his role* in the plan of redemption -- the rest of us, or those of us who were *willing*, could re-

---

[1] I Corinthians 15:21-22

[2] Isaiah 7:14

[3] Hebrews 1:6

[4] Matthew 8:27

[5] John 3:34-35

[6] Luke 1:31, Philippians 2:9-10, Hebrews 1:4.

[7] Philippians 2:8

[8] Hebrews 2:10

[9] Matthew 26:63-65

establish *our relationship* to our Heavenly Father *through him,* through an only *begotten* Son of God.

THE ONLY BEGOTTEN

So Yeshua would testify *"God so loved the world that he gave his **only begotten** Son, that whomsoever believes on him should not perish but have everlasting life."*[10] He would also testify that *"all things that the Father has are mine,"*[11] that the Son **of man** would come *"in the glory of his Father,"*[12] and that *"**the Son of man** would sit on the **right hand** of the power of God."*[13] Each of these profound and weighty statements was a declaration of *begotten Sonship* authority and dominion -- *human Sonship.*

Perhaps the clearest statement of this noble human *birthright* is in Hebrews, where it is written, *"being made so much better than the angels, as he has by **inheritance** obtained a more excellent **name** than they. For unto which of the angels said he at any time, you are my Son, this day have I **begotten** you? And again, I will be to him a Father, and he shall be unto me, a Son?"*[14] Only a *human being* would be distinguished *from the angels* in this way. God

---

[10] John 3:16
[11] John 16:15
[12] Matthew 16:7
[13] Luke 22:69
[14] Hebrews 1:4

does not have to distinguish himself from the angels, for he created them.

Further, Yeshua testified that the Father had *"committed all judgment to the Son,"* and that *"all men should honor the Son, even as they honor the Father."*[15] John the Baptist echoed that very idea when he testified that *"the Father loves the Son, and has given all things into his hand."*[16] This was a father handing the deed to the family estate to his son. This was a *delegated*, legal entrustment of authority to an *only begotten.*

But this was also the innate nobility that ultimately so offended the orthodox Jewish leaders of Yeshua's day. In fact, during Messiah's ministry the Jews *"sought the more to kill him"* because he had not only offended their idea of the Sabbath, but *"said that God was his Father, making himself **equal** with God."*[17] To them, human Sonship was an intolerable, even illegal claim.

"THE JEWS ANSWERED HIM, WE HAVE A LAW, AND BY OUR LAW HE OUGHT TO DIE, BECAUSE HE MADE HIMSELF THE SON OF GOD."

JOHN 19:7

---

[15] John 5:22-23
[16] John 3:35
[17] John 5:18

To the Jews *no man* could claim God as a literal Father and live – that was blasphemy.[18] And yet, even before Yeshua was conceived the angel Gabriel had told Mary that she would *"**conceive** in her womb, and bring forth a Son."*[19] Mary then questioned, *"How shall this be, seeing I know not a man?"*[20] And the angel answered and said unto her, *"the Holy Spirit shall come upon you, and the power of the Highest shall overshadow you: **therefore** also that holy thing which shall be born of you shall be called the Son of God."*[21]

All of this was a reference to Yeshua's *human lineage* and *birthright.* But unfortunately, since the days of Herod when news of *the birth* of the Messiah caused Herod to order the murder of all children two years old and under, Yeshua's *birthright* had been a death-sentence. It was always a stone of stumbling and rock of offense to the religious and political classes. But even so, the *conception* of Yeshua *in Mary's womb,* and all the nobility and honor that came with that conception, was a miracle -- a gift from heaven, a visitation of grace according to an *eternal purpose* to give *mankind* a new opportunity to

---

[18] Matthew 26:65
[19] Luke 1:31
[20] Luke 1:34
[21] Luke 1:35

inherit from our Heavenly Father as his *Sons and Daughters*. The conception of Yeshua brought mankind back into the family of God.[22]

THE ADOPTION

The truth is that the *principles of lineage* are part of the unseen fabric of our creation. God's order, the *Constitution* of God's Kingdom, recognizes *lineage* as the only *valid* basis for passing an *inheritance*. So it is written: *"For ye have not received the spirit of **bondage** again to fear; but ye have received the Spirit of **adoption,** whereby we cry, Abba, Father. The Spirit itself bears witness with our spirit, that we are the **children of God**: And **if** children, then **heirs;** heirs of God, and **joint heirs** with Christ; if so be that we suffer with him, that we may be also glorified together."*[23]

"If children, then heirs," is the law and logic of the universe. Consequently, *"if not children, then not heirs,"* would also follow, and our Heavenly Father didn't want that to be the outcome of his work in creating mankind. So *Adoption into* a *human lineage* that legally traced or ascended to a "Heavenly" Father was necessary in order to

---

[22] Ephesians 3:15
[23] Romans 8:15-17

legally bestow blessings that are, by nature, "*heavenly*." As it is written again, "*But when the fullness of the time was come, God sent forth his Son, made **of a woman**, made under the law, To redeem them that were under the law, that we might receive **the adoption** of sons. And **because ye are sons**, God hath sent forth **the Spirit of his Son** into your hearts, crying, Abba, Father. Wherefore thou art no more a servant, but a son; and **if a son, then an heir** of God through Christ.*"[24] And again, "*...even we groan within ourselves, waiting for the **adoption**, that is, the redemption of **our body**.*"[25]

God had it all, and *in love* he wanted to hand it down to mankind. But God's nature, the eternal principles of his own Creation and Kingdom, and *the scales of justice* that defined him as a being, demanded that man be "related" to him. Man lost *that relationship* in the Garden of Eden. But one man *found* that *relationship* again when Mary *conceived in her womb* and brought forth God's *only begotten **human** Son*. Now, through our connection and relationship with **the man** Yeshua, and through the **adoption** that brings us legally into his *human birthright*, the rest of us can become *joint heirs* with him.

---

[24] Galatians 4:4-7

[25] Romans 8:23

Seeing the end from the beginning, the ***first hint*** of this adoption was in the initial creation of man, when God said *"let **us** make man in our image, after our likeness."*[26] This statement, which was essentially a *promise,*[27] forecasted what mankind would be, not in the first Adam, not in the Adam God *knew* would fall from grace and sell his birthright -- but in a *second Adam,* the *Adam* God would appoint to *be his heir, the Adam* that would share his image and likeness, the *Adam* who would play the crucial role *with the Father* in finally making mankind into what God *intended* him to be from the beginning: *Sons and Daughters.* This *second* Adam and only *begotten* Son of God would come *from Eve,* the mother of us all.

---

[26] Genesis 1:26

[27] Titus 1:2 (God promised eternal life before the world began).

CHAPTER EIGHT

The Promised Seed

"I WILL PUT ENMITY BETWEEN YOU AND THE WOMAN, AND BETWEEN YOUR SEED AND HER SEED; HE SHALL BRUISE YOUR HEAD, AND YOU SHALL BRUISE HIS HEEL."

GENESIS 3:15

IMMEDIATELY AFTER the fall of Adam and Eve in the Garden of Eden, our Heavenly Father, *the Habitation of Justice*, designed and implemented a *dispute resolution mechanism* that would contain and ultimately resolve the dilemma presented by the two offending parties in that Garden: *Man and Angel*.

Both man and angel had sinned in the Garden of Eden. The serpent rebelled against God's universal order and purpose, and mankind fell in the process. Obviously Satan had his own agenda in tempting Eve with *the knowledge of good and evil*. He wanted something and was willing to set himself against man and God to get it. On the other hand, Adam and Eve's decision plunged the entire human race into spiritual darkness, the mind and heart of man now open to Satan's lies and deception as *death* awaited each passing generation. It was a dramatic state of affairs.

But God had a remedy, and that remedy was implemented *through his Word*. God declared a war. God set man and angel against each other in *adversarial battle* before him. God put **enmity** between the serpent and his *seed* on the one hand, and Eve and her *seed* on the other. God put it there, placed it there, set it there, and otherwise made sure it would remain there until matters that he was concerned with were eternally *resolved*. As it is written, "*I will put **enmity** between you and the woman, and between your seed and her seed; **he shall bruise your head**, and you shall bruise his heel.*"

Enmity means opposition, or to be against. This is when the serpent, a/k/a Satan, became mankind's *court-appointed adversary*[1] and *accuser*.[2] Both of these terms have a legal meaning and point to roles in a *judicial procedure*. Conversely, this is also when *prayer*,[3] petition, *advocacy*,[4] and *intercession*[5] became so relevant to man's own existence. From Genesis 3:15 forward, mankind was

---

[1] I Peter 5:8

[2] Revelation 12:10

[3] Luke 11:1-13

[4] I John 2:1

[5] Luke 21:36. *Note:* The need for prayer, and for us to pray for one another, is a Biblical theme.

summoned to come before the *Judge* and make his case, and a failure to do so would not be without consequences.[6]

Thus, in response to the *offenses* of *both* man and angel in the Garden of Eden, the *Habitation of Justice* placed himself in the role of *Supreme Judge* of an *adversarial legal battle* between them. Now, Satan would need *permission* to *test* or *cross-examine* his newly appointed opponents -- those who were aligned *against him* by God himself.[7] Similarly, from this point forward the *Judge of all the Earth* would be looking to man to stand *in the gap*[8] -- to plead, petition, and make a case on behalf of himself and his brethren.[9] This was justice. But it also had a redemptive purpose.

Because God also ruled on the *final outcome* of this *spiritual warfare*, though that outcome would take thousands of years to work itself out. God *decreed* that Eve's offspring, *her seed*, would ultimately *destroy* the works of the devil.[10] As it is written, "*it shall bruise your head.*" The Hebrew is more telling of the dimensions of God's promise. The *seed of the woman* would not merely *bruise* the serpent's head, but **crush it**, meaning a *total*

---

[6] Luke 22:31

[7] Job 1:6-12, Zechariah 3:1-7, Luke 22:31.

[8] Ezekiel 22:30

[9] Isaiah 41:21. Note: This text asks us to *make an argument* in prayer.

[10] I John 3:8

defeat of Satan's authority at the hands of *the seed of the woman, whoever* that seed may be and *whenever* that seed may come *as all creation waited.*[11]

On the other hand, God also decreed that the serpent would *bruise the heel* of the *woman's seed.*[12] This gave our adversary something to work with as he stood *against man* and tried to steal or otherwise acquire his dominion and inheritance. Adam and Eve's sin had consequences. The *seed of the woman*, and all those who would ever come to be *identified* with that *promised seed*,[13] would *suffer*, be tested,[14] and eventually bruised by a judicially-appointed adversary.[15] Of course, *Messiah's suffering* and death would be the *ultimate* fulfillment of Genesis 3:15. But *the body* of Messiah would also endure *much suffering* throughout history as well, and that suffering was also a part of God's judgment.[16] All of this was the *just response of a Holy and Almighty God* to the events in the Garden of Eden. All of human history has flowed, to a great degree, from God's *decree* in Genesis.

---

[11] Romans 8:19-23

[12] Genesis 3:15

[13] Romans 8:17, II Corinthians 1:7, I Peter 5:10, Philippians 3:10, II Timothy 2:12, 3:12.

[14] Luke 4:1-13

[15] Isaiah 50:6, Isaiah 53:5, Hebrews 2:10, I Peter 3:18.

[16] Matthew 10:22, Acts 5:41, 9:16, Romans 8:17, II Corinthians 4:1, Philippians 3:10.

Consequently, within the limits prescribed by the *Judge of All the Earth* in Genesis, Satan would make mankind's task of *re-possessing* his territory and dominion over the millennia as difficult and as costly as possible, even as he enlisted millions upon millions in the advancement of his own cause and kingdom. Satan would also seek to *devour[17]* or snuff out any hint of the *promised seed of the woman* at the earliest signs of life. Anyone showing *favor* with God or who entered into a covenant-relationship with God would become a potential target. Of course, for this Satan would need willing *agents* of his will, human vessels he could fuel with his own **enmity** against the *promised seed of the woman*. Satan's first such agent was Cain, Adam and Eve's *firstborn son*.

THE ANTICHRIST SPIRIT

Cain was essentially the first *antichrist,[18]* the first *tool* the serpent used **against** *the promised seed*, the first *brother* who murdered *brother*. As Adam and Eve's firstborn, Cain should have been *first in line* to whatever blessing or favor God had for man after the fall. But when

---

[17] I Peter 5:8

[18] *Note:* The definition of the spirit of antichrist is set forth by the Apostle John: *"every spirit that does not confess that Jesus has come in the flesh is not of God: and this is that spirit of antichrist..."* (I John 4:3). The *"flesh of Jesus"* refers to his humanity, and it begins with the *prophetic "seed of the woman."*

his younger brother Abel began to receive that favor, Cain grew jealous, even angry.[19] This jealousy became the *open door, the place* within the heart of Cain that Satan needed to further fuel Cain's resentment and hatred of Abel. This ultimately led Cain to murder his younger brother in *cold blood.*

Cain thus became the first extension of Satan's will on earth, and the story of Cain and Abel became the first manifestation of the **enmity** between the **serpent's seed** and **the seed of the woman**. As it is written, Cain was "*of that wicked one.*"[20] Yeshua would later testify that Satan was "*a murderer from the beginning.*"[21] This was a clear reference to the murder of Abel. So despite showing *favor* with God, Abel did not become or perpetuate *the heir* to *the promise.* Cain and his *spiritual father* the devil[22] made sure of that. The *seed of the serpent,* and the *spirit of antichrist,* had claimed its first victim. But this was just the first dramatic battle in a long war that would have many such casualties.

None of this went without a punishment, however. Cain was thereafter branded by God as a *criminal* and

---

[19] Genesis 4:5-6

[20] I John 3:12

[21] John 8:44

[22] Id. See Also, Matthew 13:38, 23:33.

banished from his family and his homeland.[23] And from that murderer Cain sprang the vast populations of humanity that would one day perish in Noah's flood, every imagination of their heart being only evil, continually.[24] And, according to the author of Hebrews, the *blood* of righteous Abel still *speaks* from the ground where he was killed[25] -- foreshadowing *the blood of Messiah.*

But from Abel forward, anyone who began to reflect the favor of God on their lives would be persecuted by Satan and his seed or progeny.[26] It simply came with the territory, with the *judgment of God* pronounced in Genesis 3:15. On the other hand, anyone who *resisted*[27] our adversary, who in the face of his *accusations*[28] prayed and petitioned God day and night, and who operated in faith -- could, indeed, overcome[29] the serpent. God's *scales of justice* demanded a judicial and *equitable*[30] response to all offenses in *the Garden of Eden,* and Genesis 3:15, as well as other *judgments* God would issue throughout the history of the conflict, *was that response.*

---

[23] Genesis 4:9-16.
[24] Genesis 6:5
[25] Hebrews 11:4
[26] Matthew 23:33
[27] Ephesians 4:27, 6:12, I Peter 5:8-9.
[28] Revelation 12:10
[29] Revelation 3:21
[30] Psalm 98:9, 99:4, Isaiah 11:4.

Of course, Eve went on to bear many other children with Adam, male and female, and one of her children did once again reflect the nobility of *the promise* that God had made regarding *her seed*. Eve's son *Seth* would stand in the *stead* of Abel,[31] and from Seth began the long line of succession from Eve's womb to the eventual *heir* to the promise, the **son of man**, Yeshua.[32] The lineage of the Messiah, therefore, was vital in God's *eternal purpose*. That is why *the record* of Yeshua's *lineage* is preserved in the Gospel accounts. Yeshua not only had to spring from Eve, but specifically *from Seth* and then through the long line of *promises* made to Abraham, Isaac, Jacob, and finally to David regarding his throne and kingdom. A just God required a *legal line* of succession to his throne.

But the truth is that the decreed *crushing of the serpent's head **had to be*** executed by *the seed of the woman* in God's eternal purpose and according to God's judicial and jurisprudential nature; it was the *just* requirement of a *just* God under the circumstances: *Man v. Angel*. This was the only way *mankind* could completely *re-possess* the *spiritual dominion, inheritance, and Sonship* that God had *intended* and even *set-aside* for him from the beginning. So when Mary *conceived* in her womb

---

[31] Genesis 4:25

[32] Luke 3:23-38

by the Holy Spirit,[33] the "***seed*** *of the woman*" miraculously became the *only **begotten** Son of God*. From that moment, the universe had a lawful *human* heir to "*the cattle on a thousand hills,*"[34]and so much more.[35] Similarly, when Mary conceived in her womb by the Holy Spirit, the *seed of the woman* that was to **crush** the serpent's head now became the *only **begotten** Son of God* who would destroy the works of the devil[36] and pave the way for an *adoption* and *inheritance* that staggers the imagination and stumbles the religious-minded.

"TO HIM THAT OVERCOMES WILL I GRANT TO SIT WITH ME IN MY THRONE, EVEN AS I ALSO OVERCAME AND AM SET DOWN WITH MY FATHER IN HIS THRONE."

REVELATION 3:21

It bears repeating, "*For it became him, for whom are all things, and by whom are all things, in **bringing many sons unto glory,** to make the captain of their salvation **perfect through sufferings**. For both he that sanctifies and they who are sanctified are **all of one**: for which cause he is not ashamed to call them **brethren**.*"[37] This is the key to

---

[33] Luke 1:31, 35

[34] Psalm 50:10

[35] Psalm 2:6-12

[36] I John 3:8. *Note:* Scripturally and prophetically there is a direct line from the womb of Eve to the womb of Mary; as Mary *conceives* a Son (Yeshua), the *seed* of the woman becomes God's only *begotten* Son – the man Yeshua of Nazareth.

the *eternal purpose in Yeshua*. In the foregoing text, the *"perfection through sufferings"* language flows directly from the decreed *bruising of* the heel of *the woman's seed*; the *"all of one"* and *"brethren"* language flows from *the woman* herself as our *common source* (Eve); and the *"bringing many sons unto glory"* language flows directly from God's *eternal purpose* for mankind in Yeshua -- *the seed of the woman*.

It is fundamental, therefore, that the *defeat of Satan* and of the principalities and powers that he employs, as well as the redemption of mankind and the restoration of mankind's position as a *legal heir* and *child* of God, had to be (and was *eternally designed* to be) brought about through **mankind** himself, through *the seed of the woman* – a second **Adam**, Messiah, King and High Priest -- an only **begotten** Son of God who was *at once* Eve's descendant (offspring/seed) and God's *legal heir* – as a man. This is who Yeshua really is. It is the precise combination of *"**seed** of the woman"* and "only **begotten** Son" realities in **the man** Yeshua that give him the legal *dominion and inheritance* necessary to restore **mankind** (his brethren) to Sonship and fulfill God's eternal plan.

---

[37] Hebrews 2:10-11

SPIRITUAL LIGHT

"TO THE INTENT THAT NOW, UNTO THE PRINCIPALITIES AND POWERS IN THE HEAVENLY PLACES MIGHT BE MADE KNOWN THROUGH THE CHURCH THE MANIFOLD WISDOM OF GOD, ACCORDING TO THE ETERNAL PURPOSE WHICH HE PURPOSED IN CHRIST JESUS OUR LORD."

EPHESIANS 3:10-11

Paul once prayed that the *God of Yeshua*, our Messiah, the Father of glory, would give unto each of us *the spirit of wisdom and revelation* in the knowledge of Yeshua, the eyes of our understanding being *enlightened.* He prayed that we might know the hope of God's calling, and the riches of the glory of God's *inheritance* in the saints. Paul prayed that we might know the exceeding greatness of God's power toward us who believe, according to the working of his mighty power which he revealed in Yeshua when he *raised him from the dead and set him at his own right hand in the heavens, far above all principality, power, might, dominion, and every name that is named, not only in this world, but also in that which is to come* -- putting all things under Yeshua's feet, and *giving him to be head* over a body that would fill the earth, and be filled with God.[38]

---

[38] Ephesians 1:17-23

Paul's prayer assumes a need for revelation, knowledge, and spiritual understanding. It assumes the need for enlightened spiritual eyes and spiritual wisdom. In other words, the things that Paul is asking for should not be ignored, veiled, or misunderstood. Our attention should not be directed elsewhere, to some other notion not contained in Paul's prayer to the Heavenly Father. There is a reason God preserved Paul's prayer for over two millennia.

It is *the will* of Almighty God, *the will* of our *Heavenly Father,* that believers come to know the miraculous and profound nature of Yeshua's *dominion* and *exaltation to the right hand of God* as a *second Adam*, as the promised *seed*, and as our *brother* from the same mother. Because his *inheritance* is our *inheritance*, and when we come to *that understanding*, when we *see* the true import of what God the Father has done for Yeshua of Nazareth, we can then proclaim it from the housetops to the principalities and powers in the heavenly realm – so that they understand that **we** understand *who he is* and *who we are* **in him** – *the Sons and Daughters of God Almighty.*

CHAPTER NINE

What is Man?

"WHAT IS MAN THAT YOU ARE MINDFUL OF HIM, AND THE SON OF MAN
THAT YOU VISIT HIM? FOR YOU HAVE MADE HIM A LITTLE LOWER
THAN THE ANGELS, AND CROWNED HIM WITH GLORY AND HONOR. YOU
MADE HIM TO HAVE DOMINION OVER THE WORKS OF YOUR HANDS;
YOU HAVE PUT ALL THINGS UNDER HIS FEET..."

PSALM 8:4-6

IT IS A PROFOUND question, and certainly would have been very meaningful to Yeshua, a Jew of Palestine who was careful to identify himself as **the Son of man**.[1] He knew better than anyone that man had been created in God's *image and likeness* and given *dominion* -- but *crowned* with glory and honor?

THE IMAGE OF THE HEAVENLY

Too often we look at fallen man to answer the question *what is man* -- and not to God's eternal design, plan, and purpose from the beginning. Because as it is written, *"As we have borne the image of the earthly, we shall also bear the **image** of the heavenly."*[2] And again, *"For whom he did foreknow, he did also predestine to be*

---

[1] Matthew 26:64, Mark 8:38, Luke 18:8, John 1:51, 5:27, 6:53, 12:23, 13:31.
[2] I Corinthians 15:49

*conformed to the **image** of his Son.* "[3] So what is the true image of man?

As stated earlier, from the foundation of the world God saw mankind finding his destiny, not in the first Adam, but in *the second Adam* – in Yeshua, the Messiah. As a heavenly gardener, God saw the rest of mankind as *branches* of the True Vine, as living stones in an eternal temple, and as *members* of the body[4] of his *beloved Son.* Yeshua was always the *spiritual seed, the DNA,* of what **humanity** was supposed to look like. So when Yeshua spoke of a *corn of wheat* falling into the ground and dying -- but ultimately bringing forth *much fruit* -- he was speaking not only of his own resurrection and glorification, but of *our* resurrection and glorification as well.

As the Apostle Paul would testify and teach: *"When you sow, you do not plant the body that will be, but just a **seed***, *perhaps of wheat or of something else. But God gives it a body as he has **determined**,[5] and to each kind of seed he gives its **own** body.* "[6] Paul goes on to write, *"so will it be with the resurrection of the dead. The body that*

---

[3] Romans 8:29

[4] Romans 12:5, I Corinthians 12:27, Ephesians 1:23, 4:12, Colossians 1:24, 2:19.

[5] *Note:* In this one word "determined" we have the entire *eternal purpose* of our Heavenly Father and Creator.

[6] I Corinthians 15:37-38 NIV

*is sown is perishable, it is raised imperishable; it is sown in dishonor, it is **raised in glory**; it is sown in weakness, it is raised in power."*[7]

This end-result, this glory, was *always* who and what we were in our Father's eyes – *the image* of his Son. The same God who "sees the end from the beginning" saw *the entire body* of Christ from that beginning, *raised in glory, seated in heavenly places.* God always saw the finished-product, the full-flower of his plan, *the fruit* of the *seeds* planted in Genesis, the *unpacked* DNA of creation. As it is written, *"Every plant of the field before it was in the earth, and every herb of the field before it grew."*[8] And again, *"so shall my word be that goes forth from my mouth: it shall not return unto me void, but shall accomplish that which I please..."*[9] So the *blueprint* for mankind was not what mankind looked like in his *perishable* state, but in his *eternal* state – for God is eternal.

Yeshua himself would draw on this very reality when teaching on the kingdom of God, saying *"...so is the **kingdom of God**, as if a man should cast **seed** into the ground; and he should sleep, and rise night and day, and the seed should spring and grow up, he knows not how, for*

---

[7] I Corinthians 15:42-43 NIV
[8] Genesis 2:5
[9] Isaiah 55:11

*the earth brings forth fruit of herself; first the blade, then the ear, after that the **full corn in the ear**.*"[10] And so it was from the beginning. The kingdom of God, the great tree from a single seed -- the fruit determined *by its design and purpose* – this was always the intent of the Creator for his children.

And so Yeshua testified, *"...the hour has come that the Son of man should be glorified. Truly, truly I say unto you, except **a corn of wheat** fall into the ground and die, it abides alone; but if it dies, it brings forth much fruit.*"[11] The *"much fruit"* Yeshua was referring to is his Father's *eternal purpose* for mankind *in him*. Yeshua saw **himself** as the "corn of wheat," **the seed** – but he also saw his *body* or *church* as the *ultimate bounty* of that seed. Indeed, Messiah is called the *firstfruits* of the resurrection[12] as well as the *first begotten of the dead.*[13] None of this was a mere afterthought of God's original intent in creating man, but the *Divine forethought*, the whole idea *from the beginning.*

"A GLORIOUS THRONE FROM THE BEGINNING IS THE PLACE OF OUR SANCTUARY."

JEREMIAH 17:12

---

[10] Mark 4:26-28

[11] John 12:23-24

[12] I Corinthians 15:20, 23; *See also*, James 1:18, Revelation 14:4.

[13] Revelation 1:5, Colossians 1:18

THE GLORY OF ADAM

Paul wrote that *"we all, with unveiled face beholding as in a **mirror** the glory of the Lord, are changed into the **same image** from glory to glory, even as by the Spirit of the Lord."*[14] This is who and what **we really are**. This is the design, the idea, the *eternal purpose* of our Creator -- *the **hidden wisdom** which God ordained before the world unto **our glory**.*[15] The truth is, as we have borne the image of the earthly (Adam), we will also bear the image of the heavenly (Adam).[16] And our Heavenly Father *determined* all of this before he even said *"let there be light."*

In John 17, just before going to Gethsemane, Yeshua prayed for his disciples and for all those who would ever follow him throughout history. In that prayer Yeshua made a profound statement: *"And the glory **which you have given me**, I have given them; that they may be one, even as we are one."*[17] The glory that Yeshua is referring to -- the glory that his Father had *given* him -- is none other than the glory that Yeshua had with his Father *before the world was.*[18] This was the *glory of the design **for man**,* his

---

[14] II Corinthians 3:18
[15] I Corinthians 2:7
[16] I Corinthians 15:49
[17] John 17:22
[18] John 17:5

intended glory, foreknown by the Father to be achieved first in Yeshua, and then *derivatively* by his body or church *through him*. So even as he went into Gethsemane, even as he was about to become the *"corn of wheat"* that would die to produce a *new humanity*, Yeshua was asking his Heavenly Father to allow us to share in his *eternal inheritance*. Yeshua was praying that his Father's eternal design for man would now be fulfilled in him, and that all those who believe would share in his eternal, powerful, unimaginable *foreknown* glory. And so, *what is man*?

The truth is that God had a *second, glorious Adam* tucked away, hidden from view in his foreknowledge *even as Satan plotted* the first Adam's fall. It was the image of his Son. God spoke beforehand directly to that *second and last Adam* when he said *"let us make man in our image, after our likeness."[19]* That statement was finally heard when Yeshua of Nazareth first heard it as a boy and then meditated upon it throughout his life as the ultimate *mission statement*. It spoke of a prophetic and foreordained *partnership* with his Father in bringing *many sons unto glory*.

Yeshua of Nazareth, the Messiah, Jacob's Ladder, The Beloved, the King, The High Priest, the one Mediator

---

[19] Genesis 1:26

between God and man, the seed of God's Eternal Garden and the seed of the woman -- was born to hear the message of Genesis 1:26: Let **us,** my *beloved Son* in whom I am well-pleased, my *servant* whom I uphold, the fruitful *Vine* of my garden, my *tabernacle,* my *temple,* my *express image* – let **us** make man in our image, after our likeness, and let them have dominion. This is *the relationship,* and it was the first *Messianic* prophecy. It is fulfilled when the *"corn of wheat"* (the Messiah, the Lamb of God, the second Adam)*, falls into the ground* (dies for our sins) only to *spring forth* (rise from the dead and ascend into heaven) into a glorious, *fruit-bearing tree* (God's eternal kingdom of glorified *Sons and Daughters).* In writing Genesis 1:26, the *prophet* Moses was providing Yeshua with his *mission statement* and mankind with his *eternal purpose.*

Yeshua of Nazareth knew that he was the foreknown *prototype* and *firstborn* of a *new humanity, a new creation* -- the eternal wisdom and design of God *made flesh.* Yeshua knew he was the seed *and* the fruit -- the **root** *and the* **offspring** of David.[20] As it is written, we were chosen **in him** *"before the foundation of the world, that we should be holy and without blame before him in love."*[21] And

---

[20] Revelation 5:5, 22:16
[21] Ephesians 1:4

again, *"Beloved, now are we the **sons of God**, and it does not yet appear what we shall be, but we know that when he shall appear we shall be **like him**, for we shall see him **as he is**."*[22]

This is the glory of Christ *mirrored in us* as we behold him with *unveiled* face and are changed into that same image *from glory to glory*. And this is what will happen when our Savior *reveals himself* to his *Church* as our glorified, noble, honored, exalted brother; when we behold him with *unveiled* face – when we see him **as he is.** As it is written, *"Father, I will that they also, whom you have given me, be with me where I am; that they may behold **my glory** which you have **given** me..."*[23] Here, Yeshua was praying for his own unveiling to his brethren! Paul would later remind us that even now we are *seated in heavenly places in Christ.*[24] And being there with him, now, *in this life* -- we are to **behold** his glory *as in a mirror*, and *in that glory* see what God always intended **for us!**

It is **as** the last Adam that Yeshua is the *brightness of his Father's glory and the express image of his Father's person.*[25] It is as the last Adam that Yeshua is *the image of*

---

[22] I John 3:2

[23] John 17:24

[24] Ephesians 2:6

the invisible God, the firstborn of all creation.[26] It is as the last Adam that Yeshua is the *Temple of God.*[27] It is as the last Adam that the Church of Jesus Christ should come to know and understand the glory and honor of its Messiah! For unlike what the children of Israel did with Moses, we may now behold Yeshua's glory with unveiled face -- we may now behold *the light of the knowledge of glory of God in* **the face** *of Jesus Christ* and be changed into the *same image from glory to glory by the Spirit.* This is *Sonship* -- the likeness and glory of our Father engrafted on and reflected in his children. It is also our inheritance. As it is written of man, *"you have put all things under his feet...but now we see not yet all things put under him.* ***But we see Jesus...***"[28] And again, "*the earnest expectation of the creation waits for the manifestation of* **the Sons of God.**"[29]

"AND THEY SHALL BE MINE, SAYS THE LORD OF HOSTS, IN THAT DAY WHEN I MAKE UP MY JEWELS; AND I WILL SPARE THEM, AS A MAN SPARES HIS OWN SON THAT SERVES HIM."

MALACHI 3:17

---

[25] Hebrews 1:3
[26] Colossians 1:15
[27] John 2:19
[28] Hebrews 2:8-9
[29] Romans 8:19

THE NEW JERUSALEM

So when the Apostle John recorded *his vision* of the *New Jerusalem* descending out of heaven from God adorned *as a bride* for her husband *at the end of time,*[30] we must keep in mind that this bride that John beheld was something our Creator and Heavenly Father also beheld *from the beginning of time.* It is *the fruit* of God's Garden, and the gardener knew *exactly* what *seed* to design in order to produce the fruit he desired. Similarly, when the Apostle Paul wrote that in Christ we are *the Temple of God,*[31] or that *we are built together for a **habitation of God** through the Spirit,*[32] or that the *fullness* of the God-essence dwells in Christ *bodily,*[33] we need to remember that this was God's *intended eternal purpose* for man even as he formed Adam from the dust of the earth and breathed into him the *breath of life.*[34]

All of this was the *"hidden wisdom ordained before the world to our glory."*[35] It was the *eternal life that God promised before the world began.*[36] It was God's own

---

[30] Revelation 21:10-27
[31] I Corinthians 3:16, 6:19
[32] Ephesians 2:22
[33] Colossians 2:9
[34] Genesis 2:7
[35] I Corinthians 2:7
[36] Titus 1:2

calling for mankind according to "*his own purpose and grace which was given us in Christ Jesus before the world began.*"[37] It was the *determined* design of God that we be "*conformed to the image of his Son, that he might be firstborn among many brethren*" according to *the eternal purpose* which he purposed in Christ Jesus,[38] who is, and always has been -- *the mystery of godliness* – "*revealed in the flesh, vindicated in the Spirit, beheld of angels, proclaimed among the nations, believed on in the world, and taken up in glory.*"[39]

And so it is written that we, as *living stones* in an eternal temple, "*are built upon the foundation of the apostles and prophets, Jesus Christ himself being the chief cornerstone; in whom all the building fitly framed together grows into a holy temple in the Lord: in whom you are also built together for a habitation of God through the Spirit.*"[40] This was the idea all along – a *cornerstone*, a temple built according to its *foreknown* dimensions, and an unimaginable *inheritance* for mankind.

The truth is that from the beginning of time, from the foundation of the world in the eternal design and purpose

---

[37] II Timothy 1:9
[38] Ephesians 3:11
[39] I Timothy 3:16
[40] Ephesians 2:20-22

of our all-knowing Heavenly Father -- the *last Adam,* just like the first, was never meant to be **alone.** *This reality has profound and eternal meaning for us because it means that the last Adam, our beloved Savior, was never meant to* **inherit** *alone either.* For just like the first Adam, the last Adam was always destined to be *one flesh* with his *bride.*

CHAPTER TEN

One Flesh

"FOR THIS CAUSE SHALL A MAN LEAVE HIS FATHER AND MOTHER, AND
SHALL BE JOINED UNTO HIS WIFE, AND THEY TWO SHALL BE ONE
FLESH. THIS IS A GREAT MYSTERY: BUT I SPEAK OF CHRIST AND THE
CHURCH."

EPHESIANS 5:30-32

WHEN GOD CREATED ADAM and put him in the Garden of Eden, everything was good except for one thing: Adam was alone; and in God's opinion -- that was *not good*.[1] So God caused a *deep sleep* to fall upon Adam,[2] and in that deep sleep God performed a profound and even *prophetic* surgical procedure. God opened Adam up, took out one of his ribs, and then *closed up his flesh*. The LORD God then took the rib, and out of it God made woman. God then brought the woman unto Adam.

Needless to say, Adam was pleased with what God had given him. Shortly thereafter, or perhaps immediately, Adam performed the first marriage ceremony, saying: *"This is now bone of my bones, and flesh of my flesh: she*

---

[1] Genesis 2:18
[2] Genesis 2:21

shall be called woman, because she was taken out of man. Therefore shall a man leave his father and mother, and shall cleave unto his wife, and they shall be one flesh."[3] And they were both naked, the man and his wife, and were not ashamed.[4]

THE GREAT MYSTERY

Yeshua of Nazareth would have read this first marriage story with great interest -- after all, it was actually a story about him. As it is written in Ephesians, *"we are members of his body, **of his flesh, and of his bones**. For this cause shall a man leave his father and mother, and shall be joined unto his wife, and they two shall be **one flesh**. This is a great mystery: but I speak of Christ and the church."*[5] And again, *"Husbands, love your wives, even as Christ also loved the church, and gave **himself** for it.*[6]

The truth is that all of Yeshua's statements about himself -- I am the door,[7] abide in me,[8] eat my flesh and drink my blood,[9] I am the vine and you are the branches,[10]

---

[3] Genesis 2:23-24
[4] Genesis 2:25
[5] Ephesians 5:30-32
[6] Ephesians 5:25
[7] John 10:7, 9
[8] John 15:4-5

take my yoke upon you and learn of me,[11] I stand at the door and knock,[12] upon this rock I will build my church,[13] that they may be one, even as we are one[14] -- all of these statements were made in furtherance of the full and intended meaning of Adam's prophetic statement in the Garden of Eden -- *this is now bone of my bones, and flesh of my flesh.*"[15] This, our link to the humanity of Jesus Christ, was always the *great mystery*[16] from the beginning – the *eternal purpose* of God in the Messiah, the *oneness* that both staggers the imagination and stumbles the religious minded – *one flesh* with the perfect man, the second Adam, the only begotten. It was also the very reality that was *at stake* in the *Garden of Gethsemane* and at *the Cross* – Yeshua giving *himself* so that we could be *one with him,* and he with us.

Yeshua *knew* that the only way mankind's dominion could be restored, and his brethren returned to Paradise, was for *one man* to live an entire life without sin and to then offer *himself* as a ransom payment for all those who

---

[9] John 6:53, 55-58

[10] John 15:5

[11] Matthew 11:29

[12] Revelation 3:20

[13] Matthew 16:18

[14] John 17:11

[15] Genesis 2:23

[16] Ephesians 5:32

had sinned. When this work was finished, that **one man** would then ascend to the Right Hand of God to receive an *inheritance*, an inheritance that he would then have *every right* to share with whomsoever he wished – in this case *with a bride*. Yeshua's marriage proposal couldn't be any clearer: *"I am the true Vine, and my Father is the Gardener."*[17] *"Abide in me, for without me you can do nothing."*[18] That *decreed promise* of God regarding his Son's bride had been made from the beginning. Yeshua need only ask; as it is written, *"Yet have I set my king upon my holy hill of Zion: I will declare **the decree**: the LORD has said unto me, you are my Son, this day have I begotten you. **Ask of me,** and **I will give you** the heathen for your inheritance, and the uttermost parts of the earth for your possession."*[19]

The Apostle Paul would describe the same mystery this way: *"...speaking the truth in love, we grow up into him in all things, which is the head, even Christ; from **whom** the whole body fitly joined together and compacted by that which every joint supplies, according to the effectual working in the measure of every part, makes increase of the body unto the edifying of itself in love."*[20]

---

[17] John 15:1

[18] John 15:5

[19] Psalm 2:7-8

"AND THIS IS THE RECORD: THAT GOD HAS GIVEN TO US ETERNAL LIFE, AND THIS LIFE IS IN HIS SON."

I JOHN 5:11

This is the *marriage*; this is *abiding in the Vine*; this is becoming *one flesh* with Yeshua our Savior and brother, this is partaking of *his flesh and blood*,[21] taking his yoke upon us and learning of him,[22] joining ourselves to him and becoming *one spirit* with him,[23] becoming a habitation of God through the Spirit -- in oneness with him.[24] It is also not being *ashamed* of who and what he really is, as if his humanity and his pure, holy, overcoming, noble life and identity were not enough.

All of this fulfills the promise of Yeshua's Heavenly Father regarding *his beloved Son's* inheritance in the saints, the Kingdom that had been set aside for him *and for us* in God's foreknowledge from the foundation of the world. This is an essential, even central part of the "Good News" of Yeshua's life, death, resurrection, and glorification, and we MUST come to understand it.

---

[20] Ephesians 4:15-16

[21] John 6:54, 56. Yeshua's flesh (humanity) is the *bread of life* (John 6:48) that *came down from heaven* (John 6:50-51) as the Word was *made flesh* and dwelt among us (John 1:14).

[22] Matthew 11:29

[23] I Corinthians 6:17 (*He that is joined to the Lord is one Spirit*).

[24] Ephesians 2:21-22

LEARNING OF HIM

The human mind in all its multi-layered complexity and capability is a wonderful and mysterious gift from our Heavenly Father. The mind is the portal for understanding, the translator of communication, and the interpreter of sensation and experience. The "mind" includes our thinking, our reasoning, our intelligence, our comprehension, our ideas, and to some degree our intent, purpose, and even disposition. A person's "state of mind" is an important concept in law, psychology, and medicine, and our "frame of mind" is often associated with attitude, outlook, and perspective. It is written in the scriptures that *"to be spiritually minded is life and peace."*[25] This same idea is echoed in Isaiah, where it is written: *"You will keep him in perfect peace, whose mind is stayed on you, because he trusts in you."*[26]

Our *frame of mind*, therefore, can and will affect and even dictate the translation of what we see, hear, and feel. This includes what we believe. It includes what we believe about God, about Jesus, and about ourselves. But the choice remains our own. We choose the kind of "window"

---

[25] Romans 8:6

[26] Isaiah 26:3

we look through. We choose the angles, we choose the lighting, we choose the points of reference -- all depending on what we purpose in our hearts, where we stand, what we set before us, and what we direct our attention toward. Paul even advised us to be *heavenly-minded*, to seek and set our affection on *"those things which are above, where Christ sits on the right hand of God."*[27] Again, this is a choice, a self-directed orientation, an attitude, an outlook we intentionally select. As it is written again, *"whatever things are true, whatever things are noble, whatever things are just, whatever things are pure, whatever things are lovely, whatever things are of good report, if there is any virtue and if there is anything praiseworthy—meditate on these things."*[28]

In his epistle to the Ephesians, Paul wrote about the importance of *"learning Christ,"* being *renewed in the spirit of our minds*, having a fresh mental and spiritual attitude, and *putting on the new man* which is created according to God's image.[29] This is our precise quest as believers -- to explore a renewed mind, a new way of thinking and living by "putting on" *the mind of Christ*, our glorified brother. In other words, as believers we want to

---

[27] Colossians 3:1-2

[28] Philippians 4:8

[29] Ephesians 4:20-24

look at everything, even ourselves, through *Yeshua's eyes*, think with his mind, feel with his heart, and walk in his Spirit.

Through obedience and death, Yeshua became the ladder that connects each of us to heaven *in him*. Through obedience and death, Yeshua became the link or conduit for the eternal life of God to flow *through him* into anyone who would tap in to his *human person, being, and character* -- becoming *one flesh* with him -- and in him. We take his yoke upon us and *learn of* his meekness, humility, nobility, and character. In this *fellowship*, which is symbolized in *Holy Communion*, we renew *our minds* to a different vision of ourselves *as we behold his glory*. This, in turn, transforms of our very beings. But we must first *know him*, and the power of his resurrection, and yes, even the fellowship of his suffering.[30]

So it is of great necessity, and it is our Heavenly Father's desire, that we *behold* the Son,[31] *understand* the Son, *comprehend* the Son,[32] and *see* the Son's nobility and uniqueness – as the *pattern* of what we have been ordained to be in a last, glorious and *heavenly* Adam. As it is written in Isaiah, "***Behold** my Servant, whom I uphold, my*

---

[30] Philippians 3:10

[31] John 6:40, Isaiah 42:1.

[32] Ephesians 4:13

*chosen, in whom **my soul** delights; I have put my Spirit upon him...."*[33] Yeshua himself echoed this idea when he said *"And this is the will of him who sent me; that everyone who **sees** the Son, and believes on him, may have everlasting life..."*[34] The word Yeshua used for "see" in John 6:40 literally means to behold with the *purpose* of understanding.

So as we saw in the story of Joseph, his brothers first came to him *unaware*, without knowledge, blind to the *identity* of the man who had the key to their destiny. They simply didn't recognize Joseph as their brother. But ultimately Joseph *revealed himself* to them, the veil was lifted, and the tears flowed. This was an astoundingly prophetic moment.[35] As it is written, *"Until **we all** come to the unity of the faith and of the **knowledge** of the Son of God, **unto a perfect man**, unto the measure of the stature of the fullness of Christ."*[36] According to Paul, a revelation of Christ's *perfect humanity* is the precise destiny of the Church.

---

[33] Isaiah 42:1

[34] John 6:40

[35] *Note:* In justice, Joseph's brethren were required by God to confront their own jealousy, envy, and sin in betraying Joseph even as they beheld the revelation of his exaltation. It was part of the lesson they were required to learn. So it is with Yeshua and his brethren; God will require us to face him as such.

[36] Ephesians 4:13

Until then, however, our adversary will continue his strategy to obscure the glory of his greatest nemesis, his mortal enemy, that *perfect man* of Ephesians, the *seed* of the woman, the *seed* of David, the only *begotten* Son of God and *legal heir* to all of the Father's dominion. Satan will continue to deny that Yeshua is a man, that he has *come in the flesh*, that a man could be greater and more glorious than him, because it is *the flesh, the humanity* of Yeshua, and our becoming *one flesh* with him that spells Satan's ultimate defeat – at the hands of man. So the orthodox will continue to fight against the humanity of Jesus. They will deny the real Yeshua of Nazareth and insist that he is something and someone other than who he really is.

THE END FROM THE BEGINNING

"THEN I, JOHN, SAW THE HOLY CITY, NEW JERUSALEM, COMING DOWN OUT OF HEAVEN FROM GOD, PREPARED AS A BRIDE ADORNED FOR HER HUSBAND."

REVELATION 21:2

Two Thousand years ago the Apostle John beheld the design and beauty of God's finished work, being an eye-witness to God's creative glory. John described a City, the *New Jerusalem*, otherwise known as the Church or the Body of Christ. John saw the *manifestation of the Sons and Daughters of God* descending out of heaven from God, adorned as a bride -- regal, noble, and all glorious within. Yeshua, Jesus of Nazareth, would have seen this vision as well; it would have been in his heart as he prayed in the *Garden of Gethsemane* and as he prepared his soul for the *Cross*. As it is written, it was *"for the joy that was set before him that he endured the cross, despising the shame, and is set down at the right hand of God.*[37] Yeshua's joy, Christ's joy, *was seeing the eternal purpose of his Father fulfilled.*

Jesus of Nazareth once told his disciples *"I go to prepare a place for you."*[38] That place is the finished City of God, the New Jerusalem in all its splendor, glory, and majesty. It is *the bride,* cleansed by the truth of the Eternal Word, all glorious within, a habitation for our Heavenly Father through the Spirit, a glorious Temple made up of Sons and Daughters that will one day descend out of heaven from God -- for Yeshua, for Jesus, God's only *begotten* Son – one flesh, the *eternal purpose.*

THE SCALES OF JUSTICE

We began this journey by looking through a window, a window symbolized in the *scales of justice.* That

---

[37] Hebrews 12:2
[38] John 14:2-3

window should now give us some insight into how God responded to the *foreknowledge* that Satan would deceive Eve and then lie, kill, and steal, not only to obtain *all the kingdoms of this world and their glory,* but to steal man's *inheritance* and dominion as well.

To some extent we must read between-the-lines, but whether we look at criminal law, contracts, adoption, our inheritance, the enmity, the accuser of the brethren, our advocate with the Father, our High Priest, our Mediator, or for that matter the Judge himself and eternal punishment and reward – the *scales of justice* provide an essential lens through which to view the mystery of God and of existence itself.

The same God who is the *Habitation of Justice,* who does not honor the rich over the poor, or the mighty over the weak, is the same God who, after fathering a human child and giving him his *name,* was fully willing to exalt that child to his Right Hand, willing to give that child his honor, and willing to give that child *an inheritance* fitting for who his Father really was. *God is love,* so we should not be surprised if he is *loving.* This kind of righteousness, this kind of justice, this kind of judgment, and this kind of love -- is *who* our Heavenly Father really is. God is no respecter of persons, God honors the weak and exalts the humble -- and if God is the *biological* Father of Yeshua of

Nazareth, even if that Son is *a man,* the universe MUST NOW bow its knee. It is the ultimate test of the human heart – will we see the beauty of what God has done? Remember the question:

"ARE YOU THE CHRIST, THE SON OF GOD?

Of course God would use man to defeat Satan. Of course God would Father a human Son with Mary, and of course God would honor his only begotten and beloved Son's desire for a Bride. God always intended to be our *Heavenly Father,* not just our God and Creator; and our *adoption* in Messiah was foreknown from the foundation of the world. When Yeshua offered himself without spot to God, God accepted his offering; and the *scales of justice* tipped in a way none had expected.

Yeshua's suffering and death at the hands of our adversary produced an *infinite injustice* in creation, a wrong that could not be measured; and the *Habitation of Justice* could not let that outcome be the final word of his *judicial* story. So God responded to that infinite injustice by *rebalancing the scales* – by an infinite outpouring of *grace and mercy* for anyone who would now accept the gift, and the inheritance, by confessing Jesus as Lord of all. From Messiah forward, and even retro-actively, the *Kingdom of Heaven* and *Eternal Life* was there to be re-taken by anyone with faith to overcome – by *the blood of the lamb* and the word of their *testimony*.[39] All *accusations* were rendered *irrelevant* by a simple yet profound *pardon* by the Judge of All the Universe – and who would question that pardon?

Today in our world the battle continues for the heart and soul of mankind. But Pagan Rome no longer rules the world, the Holy Bible has been the best-selling book for centuries, churches fill much of the earth, and the rule of law, human rights, *the golden rule*, and the truths of the Sermon on the Mount continue to supplant Caesars, Dictators, and Kings as the Good News of the Kingdom, and of man's redemption, continues to be preached to *all nations through the expanding footprint of the Kingdom of Heaven on Earth.* All of this *sets the stage* for what is ahead, perhaps just around the next corner.

Through the Prophet Isaiah, God told us that h*is thoughts were higher than our thoughts, and that his word, the word that came forth from his mouth,* would not return to him void, but would accomplish his *intended purpose. That Word* was Jesus, Yeshua of Nazareth, the Beloved, the Christ, the last Adam, our brother, the only begotten Son of God, our King and High Priest, our Messiah, our

---

[39] Revelation 12:11

Advocate, the Promised Seed, the Temple of God, the forethought, design, and plan of God, the expression of God, the Wisdom of God, the intended *eternal purpose* of our Heavenly Father, *the Word made flesh*, made human, made a tangible, personal *interface* through which our Heavenly Father could move and act in the *human realm* through Christ *and through his body*; and in time *all things* will be brought under ***his feet***.

"Thy kingdom come, thy will be done on earth as it is in heaven." There is a kingdom coming, *prepared from the foundation of the world for God's children*. It is our *Inheritance*. Pray for it. Believe it. Proclaim it. Wait for it. It now belongs to all of us. As it is written:

"AND NO MAN IN HEAVEN OR ON EARTH, NEITHER UNDER THE EARTH, WAS ABLE TO OPEN THE SCROLL, NEITHER TO LOOK THEREON. AND I WEPT MUCH, BECAUSE NO MAN WAS FOUND WORTHY TO OPEN AND TO READ THE SCROLL...."

"AND ONE OF THE ELDERS SAID UNTO ME, WEEP NOT: BEHOLD, THE LION OF THE TRIBE OF JUDAH, THE ROOT OF DAVID, HAS PREVAILED TO OPEN THE SCROLL, AND TO LOOSE THE SEVEN SEALS THEREOF."

REVELATION 5:3-5

WORTHY IS THE LAMB!

Amen.

EPILOGUE

The Deity of Messiah

"WHO, BEING IN THE FORM OF GOD, DID NOT CONSIDER IT ROBBERY TO
BE EQUAL WITH GOD, BUT MADE HIMSELF OF NO REPUTATION, TAKING
THE FORM OF A BONDSERVANT…"

PHILIPPIANS 2:6-7

THIS BOOK was not written to deny the Deity of Christ, but, among other things, to *explain* it. Of course, as *the only begotten Son of God*[1] and as the *Expression* of God (*Word) made flesh*,[2] Jesus Christ's human *birthright* and status was and is staggering. He is both *"form of God"* and *"equal with God,"* a seamless manifestation of our invisible[3] Heavenly Father as a perfect human Son. Jesus of Nazareth is distinguished far above all mankind and above all of the angels as well. As God's only *begotten* Son, Jesus of Nazareth is the legal and rightful heir to everything his Father owns, to *"all power in heaven and earth."*[4]

---

[1] John 3:16
[2] John 1:14
[3] Colossians 1:15, I Timothy 1:17, Hebrews 11:27.
[4] Matthew 28:18

But as the Apostle Paul described it, Jesus did not consider this *"equality with God"* something to be *grasped.*[5] Rather, being *human*, our Messiah chose to live each and every moment of his life as a humble servant. *Being found in fashion as a man*, therefore, our Messiah knew his place. The good news is -- the Father spoke to him in that place, *led* him in that place, *anointed* him in that place, *empowered* him in that place, *enlightened* him in that place, and now has *rewarded* and *honored* him in that holy, blessed, sacred place. As it is written: *"Therefore will I divide him a portion with the great, and he shall divide the spoil with the strong; because he has* **poured out his soul** *unto death..."*[6] And again, *"Behold my* **servant**, *whom I uphold,* **my elect**, *in whom my soul delights; I have put my spirit upon him..."*[7]

So our Savior found his *place in God*, not by birthright or prerogative, and certainly not by nature, but through self-denial, obedience, heart holiness, humility, and the *relationship with God that comes with an emptied, humble life.*

As a man, Jesus "grounded" the Father's power, authority, and presence on earth for the rest of us, bringing

---

[5] Philippians 2:6 NIV
[6] Isaiah 53:12
[7] Isaiah 40:1

the fullness of God into the human realm via the "perfect conduit" of his holy, sanctified, obedient human soul. Jesus *emptied himself* and was thereby *filled* with *God* -- fulfilling God's design for man that man would be a Holy Temple for God the Father to indwell by his Spirit. Jesus, therefore, was able to say *"he that has seen me has seen the Father."*[8] This is *the Deity of Messiah – the Father within him without measure.* The truth is we see the *glory of God* in the face of Jesus Christ[9] because the *fullness of the Father* dwells in Christ *bodily.*[10] This is how *the Word was made flesh.*[11] Jesus made *the eternal, invisible Father visible.*

The problem throughout Church history, however, has been the failure of orthodox religious leaders and teachers to wrap their religious minds around the idea that a man could be so distinguished, so honored by God and so worthy of *our* honor.

RELIGIOUS ORTHODOXY

Since the second and third centuries, theologians and religious people have struggled with the *humanity* of Jesus

---

[8] John 14:9
[9] II Corinthians 4:6
[10] Colossians 2:8-9
[11] John 1:14, I John 1:1-3.

and the *seamlessness* of his *relationship* with the Deity. So generations after Jesus ascended to the right hand of the Father as a *rewarded overcomer* and only *begotten* Son, the connection to his human being, identity, and person was lost. When religious people read about Christ's miracles, they saw another *person* of God. When religious people read about Christ's origins in heaven as *the Word*, the *wisdom*, and *the eternal purpose* of God, they saw another *person* of God. When religious people read about how Christ healed the sick, forgave sins, walked on water, or claimed to be "Lord of the Sabbath," they saw another *person* of God. Certainly this had to be more than a *mere man,* they reasoned.

So centuries after John lay on Christ's bosom to hear the beating of his human heart, centuries after Christ sweated drops of blood in the *Garden of Gethsemane*, and centuries after Christ was tempted on all points and *perfected through suffering*, religious-minded people forced an interpretation onto the scriptures that for hundreds of years took on the *force of law*. Christ's humanity, his human soul and identity, became an afterthought, a mere vessel or shell for who he *really* was – another *person* of God, and eventually a second of *three*.

So the real Jesus, the *human person* of Jesus of Nazareth our exalted brother, was *veiled* by religious orthodoxy. No longer would man behold *as in a mirror the glory* of the Lord and be changed into *the same image* – for Jesus was a person of God! So the *eternal purpose* of our Heavenly Father *for mankind* was veiled by blind religious orthodoxy, our inheritance remained contested by our adversary, and the manifestation of the *Sons and Daughters of God* remained on hold.

Of course, the *antichrist spirit* made the elimination of Christ's *human* identity much easier for people to accept; after all, could a man be *equal with God* – as a man? Could Sonship go that far? This was *always* the hard part, *always* the question – it had *always* been both the main threat to our adversary and the biggest stone of stumbling to the religious-minded. So through numerous religious councils and creeds the powers of orthodoxy recast and *re-branded* the Messiah over the centuries. Jesus became God, even the Creator, and the confession of this *other, more acceptable Jesus*[12] became the *litmus test* for true faith, and in some cases it meant life or death. In fact, Church history is laden with examples of believers being persecuted, and yes even killed, for not adhering to the *orthodox* position regarding who and what Jesus of Nazareth was and is.[13] The *same spirit* that caused the

---

[12] II Corinthians 11:4

[13] *Note:* From the second century forward, anyone who denied the orthodox

leaders and elders of Israel to crucify Jesus for blasphemy took up residence in institutional, organized religion and persecuted anyone who thought *a man could be equal with God* simply due to his *Sonship*. The irony of it all is staggering.

"BUT TO US THERE IS BUT ONE GOD, THE FATHER, OF WHOM ARE ALL THINGS, AND WE IN HIM; AND ONE LORD JESUS CHRIST, BY WHOM ARE ALL THINGS, AND WE BY HIM."

I CORINTHIANS 8:6

Yes, Jesus *is God* – God manifest. Jesus is *the Father with us* in and *through* a human Son. Jesus is the *wisdom* and *Word* of our Heavenly Father *expressed* in and *through* a human life. And because that's who he is, yes, he *"came down from heaven"* – just like *the Word* that came forth from our Father's mouth like the rain and snow from heaven.[14] And because that's who he, the human being is – of course the universe was *"created through him."* He was always the reason, the blueprint, the wisdom, the design of God. Jesus of Nazareth, our exalted brother, the second Adam, was and is the seed, the plan, the purpose, the spiritual DNA, the very *Constitution of Creation* as *the Word **made flesh**.

---

position has been at risk; some have been killed. Michael Servetus is a notable example.

[14] Isaiah 55:10-11

Not a single statement in the scriptures that identifies Jesus *in relationship* -- in intimate, seamless *union* or *oneness* with his Father -- was ever intended to say anything else, and the defense of orthodox teachings to the contrary will become more and more problematic as we all *"come to the unity of the faith and of the knowledge of the Son of God, unto **a perfect man**, unto the measure of the stature of the fullness of Christ."*[15]

THE WINDOW OF RELATIONSHIP

Our Savior was born to abide in his Father's heavenly love, born to be nurtured and cared for from above, born to be both presented and accepted as royalty -- even as a human being. When Mary *conceived* and God himself took on the role as the Father of her child, the universe had to stand up and take notice, and it did. This was no token or symbolic relationship. It was and is real, organic, and yes, even legal.[16]

None of the angels know or *can know* what it means to say: *"Abba, Father"* to the Creator. None of the angels, cherub or messenger, fallen or otherwise, has the *nobility, royalty or intimacy* that is *innate* to human Sonship. None

---

[15] Ephesians 4:13

[16] Hebrews 1:4 *Note*: This speaks of Yeshua's inheritance, a legal reality based in his literal Sonship.

of the angels have that distinction or that birthright; none of them know the mystery of the *Father-Son union*. God said it best: *"I will be unto him, a Father, and he will be unto me, a Son."* This is Jesus, and this is our Messiah's God[17] and Father.

From his conception[18] forward, each and every moment of our Savior's life, in every season, through thick and thin, through all the trials, joys, heartbreaks, laughter, and tears, God was *unto him* a Father and Jesus was *unto God* a Son.[19] It was and is ***a relationship***. This was the defining correlation between them ***both.*** They are a Father and a Son. That's who they are in *each other's eyes*. It is a fixed relationship vis-à-vis one another, a relationship that includes two distinct positions, roles, and identities in creation and eternity, one human, and one Divine -- each identity and role *defining* the other as *a model* for the rest of us: Father and Son, Son and Father. And this amazing *relationship*, this love that they have *for one another*, is a beautiful, wonderful, and noble thing to behold and understand – and certainly not something that someone should be persecuted for believing in!

---

[17] Revelation 3:12

[18] Luke 1:31, 35

[19] Hebrews 1:4-5

The truth is the Father *sees* Jesus through the eyes of a parent, and loves him with the heart and soul of a parent.[20] That's the Father's role, his position, his status in relation to Jesus of Nazareth. He's Christ's God, but more intimately he's Christ's Dad, his *Abba*. In fact, the word *"Father"* finds its *perfect expression* and complete meaning in the Heavenly Father's position -- as *the Father* of Jesus Christ. And, by the same token, the word *"Son"* finds its *perfect expression* and complete meaning in the position of Jesus as God's *only begotten* Son. It is the purest and most organic *relationship* in all of creation, and it is meant to be *a model* for the rest of us to learn from and even to *abide in*. It is the bridge back to *Paradise*!

We are called to see Jesus *the way* his Father sees him, to experience God's *delight* in his only *begotten* Son, to know how God feels about one man, and to see Jesus from a Father's loving perspective and let *what we behold and learn change our lives* as we realize that our Father *sees us in Jesus too*. The whole creation is waiting for this to happen so the *Sons and Daughters of God* can finally be manifest!

But we are also called to see the Father through the Son's *eyes*. After all, Jesus is the ***only man*** who has a

---

[20] Isaiah 42:1

correct and perfect perspective of God himself. Jesus *knows* God as a man, has *seen* his face, knows him *intimately*, and *understands* his power, love, and nature like no other. The *mind of Christ* is to know how a perfect man in perfect relationship with God sees himself, and God himself! As Jesus advised, *"All things are delivered unto me of my Father: and no man knows the Son, but the Father; neither knows any man the Father, save the Son, and **he to whomsoever the Son will reveal him.** "*[21]

As a second, last, and perfect Adam, Jesus *exists* to *show us the Father*. No more shame, no more hiding, no more disconnection, no more emptiness. So as the adopted *Sons and Daughters of God* we need to *tap into* the true and organic *Father-Son relationship* and partake of its *innate power* to renew our minds and transform us into what we were always intended to be. Jesus suffered and died to bridge heaven and earth! This is *abiding in the vine*, being *joined to him*, and becoming *one spirit* with him. As it is written, *"That which we have seen and heard declare we unto you, that you also may have **fellowship** with us: and truly our **fellowship** is with the Father, **and** with his Son Jesus Christ."*[22] It is precisely this fellowship,

---

[21] Matthew 11:27

[22] I John 1:3

this relationship, this communion -- that we simply MUST have. It is our inheritance!

ONE SPIRIT

"THERE IS ONE BODY, AND ONE SPIRIT, EVEN AS YOU ARE CALLED IN ONE HOPE OF YOUR CALLING. ONE LORD, ONE FAITH, ONE BAPTISM, ONE GOD AND FATHER OF ALL, WHO IS ABOVE ALL, AND THROUGH ALL, AND IN YOU ALL."

EPHESIANS 4:4-6

This fellowship with *both* the Father and his human Son Jesus is made possible by and *through the One Spirit of the Father*. As Jesus told his disciples, *"If a man loves me he will keep my words; and my Father will love him; and **we** will come and make our **abode** with him."*[23] Further, Jesus told his disciples that where two or three are gathered together, he would be in the midst of them.[24] This too, is made possible by *the Father's Spirit*.

Before his death, resurrection, and glorification, Jesus of Nazareth was in a *fixed location* as to his identity, his soul, his human person and being. But that changed when he was *glorified*, when he ascended to the right hand of his Heavenly Father. Now, *through the Spirit* of his Father, Jesus of Nazareth can *manifest himself* to anyone,

---

[23] John 14:23

[24] Matthew 18:20

anywhere, anytime -- all at once. It is part of having *all power in heaven and in earth.* As Jesus also told his disciples, *"He that has my commandments and keeps them, he it is who loves me, and he that loves me shall be loved of my Father, and I will love him, and will **manifest myself** to him."*[25] That *manifestation* is made possible by the Holy Spirit of his Father. As Peter would testify on the Day of Pentecost, *"Therefore being by the right hand of God exalted, and having **received** of the Father the **promise of the Holy Spirit**, he has now shed forth this, which you now see and hear."*[26] Jesus **received** the promise of the Holy Spirit upon his ascension into heaven! This is **how** the Lord, the last Adam, our brother manifests **himself to his church** -- via his own *union* with *the Spirit* of his Heavenly Father.

As our Savior also testified, *"A little while, and you shall not see me: and again, a little while, and you shall see me, **because** I go to the Father."*[27] And again, *"I will not leave you comfortless, **I will come unto you.**"*[28] Paul would later write, *"Now **the Lord is that Spirit**, and where the Spirit of the Lord is, there is liberty."*[29] And again,

---

[25] John 14:21

[26] Acts 2:33

[27] John 16:16

[28] John 14:18

[29] II Corinthians 3:16

*"There is **one** body, and **one Spirit**, even as you are called in one hope of your calling. **One** Lord, **one** faith, **one** baptism, **one God** and Father of all, who is above all, and through all, and **in you all**."*[30] Note the clear, *God-breathed* emphasis of the word *"one."*

When Christ was on earth, his disciples could hardly have understood how the man in front of them would be able to *manifest himself* to them and even *dwell in them* after his death. So reading through Messiah's teaching on *the Holy Spirit*, it is easy to see that he was trying to explain how this would become true after he *"went away."* The truth is, the *Holy Spirit* is the *one Spirit* of the Father, and in that o*ne Spirit* we have **fellowship** with the Father **and** with his Son.[31] After the ascension of Jesus to the right hand of God the *"Holy Spirit* of God" would thereafter be *the Father in and through the Son*, who would then be, if we accept him – also then *in us*. They, the Father and the Son *via the Spirit*, the man and his God via his Father's presence, would make *their abode* within us via that same Spirit -- and the *eternal purpose* of our Heavenly Father for mankind would be fulfilled. As it is

---

[30] Ephesians 4:4-6

[31] *Note:* The Holy Spirit is *therefore* described as someone other than the Father, or the Son, because *in the Spirit* "*he*" might or could be either, or both, depending on the moment of fellowship and which one of them is being manifest.

written, *"I in them, and thou in me, that they may be made perfect in one, and that the world may know that **thou hast loved them as thou hast loved me**."*[32]

"I in them and thou in me" – this is the Holy Spirit in the New Testament age.

THE EARNEST OF OUR INHERITANCE

The presence of the Holy Spirit in our lives, in our hearts, and in the *general assembly* or church, is also an *initial allotment* or "advance" on the greater and more expansive *inheritance* to come in eternity as God *fills* his completed Temple with his Spirit. So in the here and now we get a *foretaste* of what is to come.[33] This advance or *earnest of the Spirit* serves as a pledge or surety of God's *promise* to deliver the whole of our inheritance to us at some future time. As it is written, *"...you were sealed with that Holy Spirit of promise, which is the **earnest of our inheritance** until the redemption of the purchased possession, unto the praise of his glory."*[34] And again, *"Who hath also sealed us, and given the **earnest** of the Spirit in our hearts."*[35] And again, *"Now he that hath*

---

[32] John 14:23

[33] Hebrews 6:5: "*the powers of the world to come.*"

[34] Ephesians 1:14

[35] II Corinthians 1:22

wrought us for the selfsame thing is God, who also hath given unto us the **earnest** *of the Spirit.*"[36]

This *earnest of our inheritance* and the power and spiritual gifts that come with it was and is a *promise* of the Father from the beginning -- and hence should be made a matter of fervent petition in prayer. As it is written, *"...behold, I send* **the promise** *of my Father upon you: but tarry ye in the city of Jerusalem, until ye be endued* **with power** *from on high."*[37] And again, *"And, being assembled together with them, commanded them that they should not depart from Jerusalem, but wait for* **the promise** *of the Father, which, said he, you have heard of me. For John truly baptized with water; but ye shall be* **baptized with the Holy Spirit** *no many days hence."*[38]

The precise dimensions of this *advance* on our *spiritual inheritance* will be the subject of a future book.[39] But this profound advance is, in fact, *Christ in us,* the hope of glory.[40] It is supernatural, powerful, heavenly, and brings the Eternal Kingdom of our God into our world now, to be enjoyed as an allotment for the benefit and edification of the *body of Christ.* But know this: the

---

[36] II Corinthians 5:5

[37] Luke 24:49

[38] Acts 1:4 See Also, Acts 2:33; Ephesians 1:13.

[39] eternalpurposebooks.com

[40] Colossians 1:27.

presence of the Holy Spirit within us and among us now is part of our inheritance, part of the *eternal purpose of our Heavenly Father,* and its value cannot be measured. But that's exactly why they *tried* to get rid of Jesus of Nazareth. They wanted to *seize his inheritance,* and ours, by snuffing out who he really was. Don't let them.

The Question:
"Are you the Christ, the Son of God?"

The Answer:
"You have said; nevertheless I say unto you, hereafter you shall see the ***Son of man*** sitting on the ***right hand*** of power, and coming in the clouds of heaven."

The Verdict:
Then the high priest rent his clothes, saying, "He has ***spoken blasphemy***; what further need have we of witnesses? What think ye? They answered and said: "He is ***guilty of death***."

"But who do you say that I am?"

The End

APPENDIX

The Prophets

Inhabits Eternity - Isaiah 57:15

"For thus says the high and lofty one who inhabits
eternity, whose name *is* holy: I dwell in the high and holy
place, with him also *who* has a contrite and humble spirit,
to revive the spirit of the humble, and to revive the heart of
the contrite ones."

Virgin Birth Emmanuel – Isaiah 7:14-16

"Therefore the Lord himself will give you a sign: behold,
the virgin shall conceive and bear a Son, and shall call his
name Immanuel. Curds and honey he shall eat, that he
may know to refuse the evil and choose the good. For
before the child shall know to refuse the evil and choose
the good, the land that you dread will be forsaken by both
her kings."

A Son is Given – Isaiah 9:6-7

"For unto us a child is born, unto us a Son is given; and
the government will be upon his shoulder. And his name

will be called Wonderful, Counselor, Mighty God, Everlasting Father, Prince of Peace."

"Of the increase of h*is* government and peace t*here will be* no end, upon the throne of David and over his kingdom, to order it and establish it with judgment and justice from that time forward, even forever. The zeal of the LORD of hosts will perform this."

Israel/Jesus - Hosea 11:1

"When Israel *was* a child, I loved him, and out of Egypt I called my son."

The Peg & Glory – Isaiah 22:23-24

"I will fasten him *as* a peg in a secure place, and he will become a glorious throne to his father's house. They will hang upon him all the glory of his father's house, the offspring and the posterity, all vessels of small quantity, from the cups to all the pitchers."

The Precious Cornerstone – Isaiah 28:16-18

"Therefore thus says the Lord GOD: behold, I lay in Zion a stone for a foundation, a tried stone, a precious cornerstone, a sure foundation; whoever believes will not act hastily."

"Also I will make justice the measuring line, and righteousness the plummet; the hail will sweep away the refuge of lies, and the waters will overflow the hiding place. Your covenant with death will be annulled, and your agreement with death will not stand; when the overflowing scourge passes through, then you will be trampled down by it."

The Branch/Root of David – Isaiah 11:1-4

"There shall come forth a rod from the stem of Jesse, and a branch shall grow out of his roots. The Spirit of the LORD shall rest upon him, the Spirit of wisdom and understanding, the Spirit of counsel and might, the Spirit of knowledge and of the fear of the LORD."

"His delight *is* in the fear of the LORD, And he shall not judge by the sight of his eyes, nor decide by the hearing of his ears; but with righteousness he shall judge the poor, and decide with equity for the meek of the earth; he shall strike the earth with the rod of his mouth, and with the breath of his lips he shall slay the wicked."

The Arm of the LORD – Isaiah 40:9-11

"O Zion, you who bring good tidings; get up into the high mountain; O Jerusalem, you who bring good tidings, lift up your voice with strength, lift *it* up, be not afraid; say to the cities of Judah, behold your God! Behold, the Lord GOD shall come with a strong *hand,* and his arm shall rule for him; behold, his reward *is* with him, and his work before him. He will feed his flock like a shepherd; he will gather the lambs with his arm, and carry *them* in his bosom, *and* gently lead those who are with young."

The Arms of the LORD - Isaiah 51:5

"My righteousness *is* near, my salvation has gone forth, and my arms will judge the peoples; the coastlands will wait upon me, and on my arm they will trust."

Arm of the LORD/Servant- Isaiah 52:10, 13, 14

"The LORD has made bare his holy arm in the eyes of all the nations; and all the ends of the earth shall see the salvation of our God."

"Behold, my servant shall deal prudently; he shall be exalted and extolled and be very high."

"Just as many were astonished at you, so his visage was marred more than any man, and his form more than the sons of men."

Arm of the LORD/Servant- Isaiah 53:1-12

Who has believed our report? And to whom has the arm of the LORD been revealed?

"For he shall grow up before him as a tender plant, and as a root out of dry ground. He has no form or comeliness; and when we see him, *there is* no beauty that we should desire him."

"He is despised and rejected by men, a man of sorrows and acquainted with grief. And we hid, as it were, *our* faces from him; he was despised, and we did not esteem him."

"Surely he has borne our grief and carried our sorrows; yet we esteemed him stricken, smitten by God, and afflicted."

"But he *was* wounded for our transgressions, *he was* bruised for our iniquities; the chastisement for our peace *was* upon him, and by his stripes we are healed."

"All we like sheep have gone astray; we have turned, every one, to his own way; and the LORD has laid on him the iniquity of us all."

"He was oppressed and he was afflicted, yet he opened not his mouth; he was led as a lamb to the slaughter, and as a sheep before its shearers is silent, so he opened not his mouth."

"He was taken from prison and from judgment, and who will declare his generation? For he was cut off from the land of the living; for the transgressions of my people he was stricken."

"And they made his grave with the wicked, but with the rich at his death, because he had done no violence, nor *was any* deceit in his mouth."

"Yet it pleased the LORD to bruise him; he has put *him* to grief. When you make his soul an offering for sin, he shall see h*is* seed, he shall prolong h*is* days, and the pleasure of the LORD shall prosper in his hand."

"He shall see the labor of his soul, *and* be satisfied. By his knowledge my righteous servant shall justify many, for he shall bear their iniquities."

"Therefore I will divide him a portion with the great, and he shall divide the spoil with the strong, because he poured out his soul unto death, and he was numbered with the transgressors, and he bore the sin of many, and made intercession for the transgressors."

The Arm of the LORD - Isaiah 51:9-10

"Awake, awake, put on strength, O arm of the LORD! Awake as in the ancient days, in the generations of old. *Are* you not *the arm* that cut Rahab apart, *and* wounded the serpent? *Are* you not *the* one who dried up the sea, the waters of the great deep; that made the depths of the sea a road for the redeemed to cross over?

Arm of the LORD - Isaiah 59:16

"He saw that *there was* no man, and wondered that *there was* no intercessor; therefore his own arm brought salvation for him; and his own righteousness, it sustained him."

God's Right Hand - Isaiah 48:13

"…my hand has laid the foundations of the earth, and my right hand has spanned the heavens."

God's Servant/Elect – Isaiah 42:1, 6

"Behold! My servant whom I uphold, my elect one *in whom* my soul delights! I have put my Spirit upon him; he will bring forth justice to the Gentiles."

"I, the LORD, have called you in righteousness, and will hold your hand; I will keep you and give you as a covenant to the people, as a light to the Gentiles…"

Anointed One - Isaiah 61:1-3

"The Spirit of the Lord GOD *is* upon me, because the LORD has anointed me to preach good tidings to the poor; he has sent me to heal the brokenhearted, to proclaim liberty to the captives, and the opening of the prison to *those who are* bound; to proclaim the acceptable year of the LORD, and the day of vengeance of our God; to comfort all who mourn, to console those who mourn in Zion, to give them beauty for ashes, the oil of joy for mourning, the garment of praise for the spirit of heaviness; that they may be called trees of righteousness, the planting of the LORD, that he may be glorified."

God's Servant - Isaiah 49:1-3

"Listen, O coastlands, to me, and take heed, you peoples from afar! The LORD has called me from the womb; from the matrix of my mother he has made mention of my name. And he has made my mouth like a sharp sword; in the shadow of his hand he has hidden me, and made me a polished shaft; in his quiver he has hidden me. And he said to me, 'you *are* my servant, O Israel, in whom I will be glorified."

Eternal Purpose - Isaiah 51:16

"And I have put my words in your mouth; I have covered you with the shadow of my hand, that I may plant the heavens, lay the foundations of the earth, and say to Zion, you *are* my people."

Word/Seed - Isaiah 55:9-11

"For *as* the heavens are higher than the earth, so are my ways higher than your ways, and my thoughts than your thoughts. For as the rain comes down, and the snow from heaven, And do not return there, but water the earth, and make it bring forth and bud, that it may give seed to the sower and bread to the eater, so shall my word be that goes forth from my mouth; it shall not return to me void, but it shall accomplish what I please, and it shall prosper *in the thing* for which I sent it."

The Messiah - Isaiah 50:4-9

"The Lord GOD has given me the tongue of the learned, that I should know how to speak a word in season to *him who is* weary. He awakens me morning by morning; he awakens my ear to hear as the learned. The Lord GOD has opened my ear; and I was not rebellious, nor did I turn away."

"I gave my back to those who struck m*e,* and my cheeks to those who plucked out the beard; I did not hide my face from shame and spitting."

"For the Lord GOD will help me; therefore I will not be disgraced; therefore I have set my face like a flint, and I know that I will not be ashamed. *He is* near who justifies me; who will contend with me? Let us stand together. Who *is* my adversary? Let him come near me. Surely the Lord GOD will help me; who *is* he *who* will condemn me? Indeed they will all grow old like a garment; the moth will eat them up."

Contrite Spirit - Isaiah 66:2

"For all those *things* my hand has made, and all those *things* exist," says the LORD. But on this *one* will I look: On *him who is* poor and of a contrite spirit, and who trembles at my word."

Foreknowledge - Jeremiah 1:5

"Before I formed you in the womb I knew you; before you were born I sanctified you; I ordained you a prophet to the nations."

The Branch - Jeremiah 23:5-6

"Behold, *the* days are coming," says the LORD, that I will raise to David a branch of righteousness; a King shall reign and prosper, and execute judgment and righteousness in the earth. In his days Judah will be saved, and Israel will dwell safely; now this *is* his name by which he will be called: The LORD our Righteousness."

The Branch - Jeremiah 33:15-22

"In those days and at that time I will cause to grow up to David a branch of righteousness; he shall execute judgment and righteousness in the earth. In those days Judah will be saved, and Jerusalem will dwell safely. And this *is the name* by which she will be called: The LORD our Righteousness."

"For thus says the LORD: David shall never lack a man to sit on the throne of the house of Israel; nor shall the priests, the Levites, lack a man to offer burnt offerings before me, to kindle grain offerings, and to sacrifice continually."

"And the word of the LORD came to Jeremiah, saying, Thus says the LORD: If you can break my covenant with the day and My covenant with the night, so that there will not be day and night in their season, then my covenant may also be broken with David my servant, so that he shall not have a son to reign on his throne, and with the Levites, the priests, my ministers. As the host of heaven cannot be numbered, nor the sand of the sea measured, so will I multiply the descendants of David my servant and the Levites who minister to me."

The Majestic Cedar - Ezekiel 17:22-24

"Thus says the Lord GOD: I will take also *one* of the highest branches of the high cedar and set *it* out. I will crop off from the topmost of its young twigs a tender one, and will plant *it* on a high and prominent mountain. On the mountain height of Israel I will plant it; and it will bring forth boughs, and bear fruit, and be a majestic cedar. Under it will dwell birds of every sort; in the shadow of its branches they will dwell. And all the trees of the field shall know that I, the LORD, have brought down the high tree and exalted the low tree, dried up the green tree and made the dry tree flourish; I, the LORD, have spoken and have done *it*."

The Soul of the Son - Ezekiel 18:4

"Behold, all souls are Mine; the soul of the father as well as the soul of the son is mine; the soul who sins shall die."

The Gap - Ezekiel 22:30-31

"So I sought for a man among them who would make a wall, and stand in the gap before me on behalf of the land, that I should not destroy it; but I found no one. Therefore I have poured out my indignation on them; I have consumed them with the fire of my wrath; and I have recompensed their deeds on their own heads, says the Lord GOD."

The Shepherd - Ezekiel 34:23-24

"I will establish one shepherd over them, and he shall feed them, my servant David. He shall feed them and be their shepherd. And I, the LORD, will be their God, and my servant David a prince among them; I, the LORD, have spoken."

The Prince - Ezekiel 44:1-3

"Then he brought me back to the outer gate of the sanctuary which faces toward the east, but it *was* shut. And the LORD said to me, this gate shall be shut; it shall not be opened, and no man shall enter by it, because the LORD God of Israel has entered by it; therefore it shall be shut. *As for* the prince, *because* he *is* the prince, he may sit in it to eat bread before the LORD; he shall enter by way of the vestibule of the gateway, and go out the same way."

The Branch - Zechariah 6:12-13

"Then speak to him, saying, thus says the LORD of hosts, saying: behold, the man whose name *is* the BRANCH! From his place he shall branch out, and he shall build the temple of the LORD; yes, he shall build the temple of the LORD. He shall bear the glory, and shall sit and rule on his throne; so he shall be a priest on his throne, and the counsel of peace shall be between them both."

The Price - Zechariah 11:12

"Then I said to them, if it is agreeable to you, give *me* my wages; and if not, refrain." So they weighed out for my wages thirty *pieces* of silver."

The Son of God - Zechariah 12:10

"And I will pour on the house of David and on the inhabitants of Jerusalem the Spirit of grace and supplication; then they will look on me whom they pierced. Yes, they will mourn for him as one mourns for *his* only *son,* and grieve for him as one grieves for a firstborn."

The Shepherd - Zechariah 13:6-7

"And *one* will say to him, what are these wounds between your arms? Then he will answer - *those* with which I was wounded in the house of my friends."

"Awake, O sword, against my shepherd, against the man who is my companion, says the LORD of hosts. Strike the shepherd, and the sheep will be scattered; then I will turn my hand against the little ones."

The Second Coming - Zechariah 14:3-5, 9

"Then the LORD will go forth and fight against those nations as he fights in the day of battle. And in that day his feet will stand on the Mount of Olives, which faces Jerusalem on the east. And the Mount of Olives shall be split in two, from east to west, m*aking* a very large valley; half of the mountain shall move toward the north and half of it toward the south."

"Then you shall flee *through* my mountain valley, for the mountain valley shall reach to Azal. Yes, you shall flee as you fled from the earthquake in the days of Uzziah king of Judah. Thus the LORD my God will come a*nd* all the saints with you."

"And the LORD shall be King over all the earth. In that day it shall be: The LORD *is* one and his name one."

The Messenger - Malachi 3:1-3

"Behold, I send my messenger, and he will prepare the way before me. And the Lord, whom you seek, will suddenly come to his temple, even the messenger of the

covenant, in whom you delight. Behold, he is coming,
Says the LORD of hosts."

"But who can endure the day of his coming? And who can
stand when he appears? For he *is* like a refiner's fire and
like launderer's soap. He will sit as a refiner and a purifier
of silver; he will purify the sons of Levi, and purge them
as gold and silver, that they may offer to the LORD an
offering in righteousness."

The Sun of Righteousness - Malachi 4:2-6

"But unto you that fear my name shall the Sun of
righteousness arise with healing in his wings; and you
shall go forth, and grow up as calves of the stall."

"And you shall tread down the wicked; for they shall be
ashes under the soles of your feet in the day that I shall do
this, says the LORD of hosts."

"Remember the law of Moses my servant, which I
commanded him in Horeb for all Israel, with the statutes
and judgments."

"Behold, I will send you Elijah the prophet before the
coming of the great and dreadful day of the LORD; and he
shall turn the heart of the fathers to the children, and the
heart of the children to the fathers, lest I come and smite
the earth with a curse."

Made in the USA
Charleston, SC
07 April 2014